Parenting Kids That Are Respectful, Responsible, and Obedient

Don Jacobsen

Published by HighWalk Productions Inc.

www.RareKidsWellDone.com

Author: Don Jacobsen
1donj@earthlink.net

Editor
Lori Peckham

Cover and Content Design
Harding Design

ISBN: 978-1-4507-3652-7

CONTENTS

[FOREWORD]

As I read through the tens of thousands of titles listed under the subject of "Parenting" at the Amazon.com website I discover something interesting: There are not very many of those authors I agree with, although I have to admit that doesn't bother me a whole lot.

Kevin Leman is one; he and I breathe the same air. James Dobson and I agree on most of the significant issues regarding how to raise kids. There are others, but not many.

But now there is another. My friend and colleague, Don Jacobsen, has done a great job of capturing what I believe are the essentials of love and leadership parenting in his book, Rare Kids; Well Done.

This is a great book – you'll love it! It's well illustrated from real life and filled with keen insights, apt humor, and wise counsel. It's a family-changer. I'm glad to see the library of books available to parents expanding, especially when they deal – as this one does - with traditional values, parent-centered families, and character-centered parenting.

John Rosemond
Gastonia, NC
March 2011

SURPRISE!

I think I thought it would be easy. I mean, by the time we got the "nursery" ready we figured the most difficult task facing us was choosing a name that both sets of grandparents could live with (and not write us out of their will). Sure, there would be a few nights of slightly interrupted sleep till the baby got in sync with our schedule, but with his food supply at a constant of 98.6°, that wasn't going to be especially disruptive to my sleep patterns.

Yeah, right.

I don't remember if it was the first night home from the hospital or the second, but sometime early in that sequence we discovered that this guy was going to mow his own swath across our field. I mean, he had no concern for our schedule. We wanted to sleep, and he wanted to eat—we fed him. We wanted to run an errand, but it was his bath time—he got a bath. We wanted to jump in the car and go visit the grandparents—we packed for hours before leaving. (Do you know how much stuff it takes to maintain a baby on the road for a weekend? And that was before car seats! And do you know how much volume it adds to the stuff in your trunk when the baby graduates to bottles?)

Is it possible that I had underestimated the investment this project was going to require? That was the steepest 72-hour learning curve I have ever encountered. Ugh.

Yet I would learn that this was the easy part. It would be a half dozen years before *he* would be enrolled in school. *My* education had already begun.

I never went to "How to Bring Up Kids" school and never took a course in "Babies 101." I've got a bunch of degrees, but none of them prepared me for what I had just been at least partly responsible for creating. That was one of my most humbling revelations. I call it the era of my Ph.D., when I got my "**P**retty **h**arried **D**ad" degree. It's the toughest one I ever got—and the most rewarding.

I don't remember the moment—it was more like a dawning awareness, I think—when it occurred to me that I had been entrusted with a little person who was in many ways a blank canvas. Impressionable. Absorbent. Pliant.

Now, that ups the ante. Keeping him housed, fed, bathed, clothed, healthy… those are the easy projects. If nothing else, those are social norms. Do them, or someone from Child Protective Services will come bang on your door.

But what about the big issues: honesty, caring, unselfishness, purity, respect, industry, loyalty? You and I could both make a long list. Where do *those* come from? They are not in the DNA. I learned that they are taught. And caught.

That reality got my attention. Multiplication tables he would get at school. Sportsmanship would be emphasized at Little League. We could hire a Driver's Ed teacher. He could ride his bike down the street to a piano lesson. But the other stuff—the big stuff, the important stuff, the truly consequential stuff—that would be the responsibility of his mom and me. Not the church, not the school, not the state, not his peers. They might help, but the responsibility was *ours*.

It hit me: Parenting isn't rocket science—it's harder than that.

Rockets respond to the laws of physics. Kids don't. Rockets tend to be pretty predictable. Kids aren't. Rockets can be programmed. Kids can't. If you get it right with one rocket, the next one will likely follow the same trajectory. Not so with kids.

I also learned that I couldn't back out on this venture. I was irrevocably committed to the long haul.

Now what?

That's why I wanted to write a book. This is a "Now what?" book.

This is what I wish I had known before I learned what I know. I learned a lot of stuff in grad school that I didn't need to know. In fact, I learned a lot of stuff in grad school that I later learned wasn't so. (That got a little poetic, didn't it?) If I hadn't thought that stuff was true, life would have been a lot easier for our two kids—and for both of their parents. It took me a long time to unlearn it.

I am not an authority; no parent in their right mind would make that irresponsible claim. But I am a veteran (small v). I have two kids, both in their second half-century of life, and two of the world's most beautiful granddaughters. (Don't challenge me on that—I can get ugly.)

I am also married to—as I often tell her—the world's most incredible grandmother. That doesn't make me an authority either, but it does mean that I've had a delightful partner on this journey.

So, shall we begin?

Oh, I should probably mention that by the time you read this I may be a great granddad. Now, that'll age ya!

Next page, please . . .

CHAPTER 1

THE NEW 3 R'S OF LEADERSHIP PARENTING:

Raising Kids That Are Respectful, Responsible, and Obedient

OK, this really should be called *Raising Kids That Are Respectful, Responsible, and Resolute,* or something like that. But because I couldn't find a word that means obedient that begins with an "R" (even though I read clear through the "R" section of my dictionary), I decided I'd have to settle for obedient.

Then I thought, *Hey, look at the stretch they had to go to in order to get the first three R's, right?* I mean, look at this: *reading, writing,* and *arithmetic.* There's hardly an R in the list. You have to be really creative to get three R's out of *that.* Mine is closer than the original—at least I got two out of three.

See, in my vocabulary "resolute" is really not big enough to encompass what we need to talk about. So even if I had used some other word, it would have come out looking a lot like obedient. So I decided to just say it like it is.

RESPECTFUL

Somebody's been eavesdropping on our front porch.

As I talk to parents around the country, often one of the first concerns I hear expressed goes something like this: "Dr. Don, how can I get my kids to treat me with respect? I mean, they talk back; they roll their eyes. They use words my folks would have killed me for when I was young. When I tell them to do something, they often defy my instructions. They don't honor the curfews I set, and when I get on them about it, they pitch a fit, call me awful names, and slam the door. And they give me this dumb comment: 'Whatever . . .'"

Now, maybe the conversation isn't that shrill at your house, but you won't have to go very far down the block before you could show that paragraph to a dad or mom and they would say, "Somebody's been eavesdropping on our front porch."

You and I didn't grow up that way. What happened? Maybe we

can blame it on our kids' peers—I'll bet that's it. Or maybe television sitcoms? Don't you wish it were that easy to diagnose—and solve?

Let's see if we can pry the lid off this ugly box.

Rudeness is a weak person's imitation of strength.

Rudeness is a weak person's imitation of strength. Our kids show rude when they begin to sense that their world is not holding still; it's screaming past, and they don't have much say about what's going on. They often look at the authority figures in their lives—teachers, parents, stepparents, police, politicians—and they aren't sure they are always getting wise counsel, good advice, dependable examples, trustworthy information, sound judgment, or strong boundaries.

A lot of what's going on around them is broken, and they don't like the feel of that, especially since they can't fix it. Part of the disrespect grows out of disappointment. Part of it from anger. Part of it from fear.

Let me see if I can describe at least part of the parental conduct that helps restore a child's confidence and builds respect—and some of what we're going to be working on:

- Respect is a street with two-way traffic. We all, kids included, tend to show respect to those who respect us. Treat your kids with the same courtesy as you do your best friend.

- As a parent, you are the leader in your family. Not a despot, but the leader. Not a wimp, but the leader. There should be few rules, with obedience anticipated. The kids are free to disagree, but they are not free to disobey. If they choose to disobey, there will be consequences. It's predictable. Life is like that. A family is a kid's preparation for life.

- Your children will become like you are, so be what you want them to be. No shortcuts here, no games. Kids are God's little spies—they'll know. Personal integrity is huge. No one can spot a phony like a kid, and nobody respects a phony.

- Engulf your kids in genuine affirmation. Pay them honest compliments. Look for traits in them that they may not notice in themselves. Not flattery, but honest appreciation. Don't exaggerate, but look for reasons to commend them.

- Listening is a learned skill. Learn it well. Reflect back to them what you think you are hearing them say. "I'd love to hear what your thinking is on the subject of . . ." is a great and respectful way to begin a conversation. Then don't argue or refute; just listen. There are few things you can do that will demonstrate respect more powerfully.

- Lead your family in looking for people you can help. You'll get more respect from your kids if you help *others* than if you help *them*. This trait grows out of a *gratitude mind-set* rather than an *entitlement mind-set*. As a bonus, few activities build *self-respect* better than this one because it goes beyond today's self-help hype of knowing what you want and how to get it to knowing what you have and how to give it.

- Never argue with your kids. Never. Not ever. How do you live by *that* rule in the real world? We'll talk about it more later, but it's so important that I wanted to get it on this list as an essential.

This first R is so important that we've got to get it right. It'll show up all the way through the book . . . and all the way through life.

RESPONSIBLE

Boy, are those experts wrong.

There is a general sense among a lot of parents and among those who deal with mental health issues in America that the teen years represent the time for kids to kick up their heels and party, because the time will come soon enough when they will need to settle down and become productive citizens.

By many, the teen years are described as incurably irresponsible and childish. The argument is often made that adolescents are hormonally and genetically programmed to bizarre behaviors. So don't worry when your kids do dumb stuff, the experts entreat, because your kids have to go through this crazy spell; it's in their genes. They can't help it. Don't expect self-discipline, compassion, acts of unselfishness, or examples of your children intentionally inconveniencing themselves on behalf of others.

Boy, are those experts wrong.

But isn't it kind of inescapable? I mean, there is this mismatch between their physical development and their emotional maturity, right? Hormones and all that stuff, you know. Shouldn't we give them a pass till they climb fools' hill? Shouldn't they be footloose and fancy-free in their teens because reality is just around the corner?

A recent book on parenting argues that we don't dare expect too much from our teens because they're crazy anyway. The author, Michael Bradley, states:

> Be a little understanding. These are often terrible times for your kid. He is probably brain-challenged, overwhelmed with irresolvable conflicts, and forced to constantly see mostly his failures. Your daughter is nuts and she's scared of not looking right, sounding right, or even thinking right. As such, she requires special handling. Just trying to have a conversation with a teen caught in the crush of adolescent dysfunction can be an art form.[1]

Oh, I get it; we don't dare expect too much sanity from our kids; they can't be expected to be in control of their actions or attitudes at

1   Michael J. Bradley, Yes, Your Teen Is Crazy! (Harbor Press, 2003), p. 12.

this time in their lives. No wonder they talk to us like they do—it's not their fault. As if to leave no question in our minds about his thesis, the author continues: "You can't just be natural with your troubled teen. That's because he's nuts."[2] No wonder he titled his book *Yes, Your Teen Is Crazy!*

Being a kid is not an idea that is new to this century. They've been around for a long time. I was one once; likely you were too. I fear that Dr. Bradley has a distorted view of history. He cites research that the human brain is actually in a developmental stage till the age of 20 (as though that were some kind of new phenomenon). If it were, we would expect that all through history adolescents would have been prey to these same mental and emotional aberrations.

If the condition is truly endemic to the age-group, what changed? History, in fact, challenges that assumption. Historian Friedrich Heer recounts how in 1800s Europe it was not uncommon for boys to join the Prussian Army as officer cadets at the age of 15. University entrance was common at 15 and 16. In this country, George Washington was hired as a surveyor (think trigonometry and calculus) at the age of 17. When he was 12, David Farragut was given command of a ship *and crew* by the U.S. Navy. At 17, Clara Barton was a successful schoolteacher with 40 students in her class—some of them as old as she was.

Do you know the name Alexis de Tocqueville? He was a brilliant French nobleman-scholar who came to America in the early 1830s to study this new experiment in democracy. The books that came from his research are still classics more than 150 years later. Very little escaped de Tocqueville's notice. He carefully describes a young nation where its youth are responsible, involved, thoughtful, and very much a part of their communities. What changed from then to now?

It can be readily argued that the culture was markedly different in early nineteenth-century America than it is today and these were family expectations. No argument there, but my question is: Where were the hormones? Where was the anger? And the tantrums?

---

2   *Ibid*, p. 14.

In *Do Hard Things*, a wonderful book by the precocious teenage twins, Brett and Alex Harris, is this interesting summary:

> People today view the teen years through the modern lens of adolescence . . . that allows, encourages, and even trains young people to remain childish for much longer than necessary.[3]

Granted, these authors are not authorities, but you have to admit that they are pretty astute observers. Incidentally, they are the organizers of a movement that is strong and growing in the youth culture, which they call a "Rebelution." It is a response to their concern that America is afflicting its youth with an atmosphere of low expectations. They'd like to do something about that.

Responsibility is a learned skill. It is neither congenital nor automatic.

At what age are you asking your kids to become responsible for a growing list of chores? During their third year, I hope. Responsibility is a learned skill. It is neither congenital nor automatic. It's a habit that develops through practice. And as a friend of mine likes to say, "Home is where our story begins."

OBEDIENT

The third of the three desirable characteristics we seek to instill in our children is obedience. In a permissive culture such as ours, the very word "obedience" instantly raises the blood pressure of some. It smacks of oppression and control, manipulation and coercion. But in any functioning entity the members must respond appropriately to the rightful authority figures or there is chaos.

---

3   Alex and Brett Harris, *Do Hard Things* (Multnomah, 2008), p. X.

The citizens of this free nation cannot set their own speed limit on the highway. A person convicted of a crime is not free to determine whether or not he will accept the sentence. A person is not allowed to enter a Denver Bronco's football game without a ticket. If you check a book out of the library, it is not optional whether or not you return it. In every facet of our lives we are subject to appropriate authority. Otherwise the organization self-destructs.

Thus it is with the family.

I probably couldn't get 100 percent agreement on this, but it is true nonetheless: A 35-year-old mom knows more about what is best for a 9-year-old third-grader than the 9-year-old third-grader does. If the 9-year-old third-grader—or the 15-year-old sophomore—decides that he/she is going to disregard those who are in rightful authority and make his/her own decisions, it compromises the strength of the family, and it lays the groundwork for serious relationship problems in the future for the youngster.

The decade of 3-to-12 is what my colleague, John Rosemond, calls the decade of discipline. Incidentally, discipline is not a synonym for punishment. Discipline comes from "discipling," teaching, nurturing a follower. Pre-3, obedience is only a delicious dream. Beginning at 3, and lasting about 10 years, is that window during which we are obligated, for our sake, for the child's, and for the community's, to disciple and teach and nurture.

**"Because I said so and I'm the mommy (or daddy)"
is an acceptable answer.**

"Few rules" is the rule. Simple, but enforced. "Because I said so and I'm the mommy (or daddy)" is an acceptable answer. You are the rightfully constituted authority. Any teacher will tell you that your child will do better in school if when they arrive there they are experienced at responding well to authority. Any employer will tell you that the new hire who listens and is respectfully responsive to those in charge will do better.

So, building kids that are respectful, responsible, and obedient . . . Tall order. Big assignment. Challenging project . . . But that's what this book is for. Read on.

THEY BROKE THE MOLD

The most important decision you ever made was to have kids.

Really?

A lot of people think so.

How so?

No one in history has ever had, nor will ever have, a child just like yours.

Well, when you made the decision to have children, you decided to participate in birthing a brand-new living person onto the planet . . . a little person who had never existed before. One of a kind. There had never been nor will there ever again be a person just like your baby. You and your spouse contributed a unique combination of DNA that was unlike any other that would ever exist. No one in history has ever had, nor will ever have, a child just like yours. When your youngster showed up, they broke the mold.

Some children grow up and change the world. Perhaps yours will too. One baby grew up and developed penicillin. One baby grew up and made the first trip into space. One baby grew up and discovered the North American continent. One baby grew up and showed the world that even wounded soldiers could be nursed back to health. One baby grew up and made it possible for every home to have electricity. One baby grew up and gave us the "Hallelujah Chorus." One baby grew up and gave us a dictionary that defines every word in our language. One baby grew up and taught us 266 things we could make out of peanuts.

Not all world-changers have their names in history books. One baby grew up and taught a roomful of inner-city underachievers how to read. One baby (whose name you probably don't know, nor do I) grew up and three generations later a baby was born from her family and grew up to become president of the United States and challenged the evils of slavery.

How will your kids change the world? Who knows? We still need a cure for cancer. We still need great educators. We still need someone to help us establish peace among the nations. We still need someone to help us eliminate hunger on a planet that has plenty for all. We still need someone to show us how to manage our energy resources. We still need someone to help us restore morality and integrity to our culture.

You're suggesting that my son can help change the world? The fact is, he can't even remember to change his socks.

Our world needs your kids!

"Let me get this straight, Dr. Don . . . You're suggesting that my son can help change the world? The fact is, he can't even remember to change his socks."

"My daughter help change the world? I can't even get her to signal when she changes lanes in traffic."

"My kids help to make the world a better place? I can't even get them to make their beds."

Don't panic—and don't scoff. You have the privilege of helping that youngster become. You have the joy of helping them discover why they were put here. You have the assignment of creating a setting in which he can achieve his maximum potential. You have the task of coaching her through the unpredictable, scary process of moving from spectator to participant.

You are watching for strengths in them they don't see in themselves. It's up to you to coach them toward greatness . . . and to believe it's possible. It's up to you to help inspire the dreams they will dream, and then help nurture those dreams. It's up to you to look beyond all the things they can't do and help them envision all the things they can learn to do.

"But it isn't just up to me," you argue. "That's why they go to school, right?" OK, but by the time they finish sixth grade, they will have spent 6,000 hours in school and 60,000 hours at home. Do the math.

So get past the zits, the messy room, the self-doubt, the creepy friends, the trendy clothes, the desire to tattoo or pierce every place that shows and some that don't, and see in your youngster a potential world-changer who has come to live at your house. And you signed on as coach, mentor, role model, and talent scout.

Think about it: Kids from our generation will surface as leaders in every field. Every field. Technology, government, medicine, the arts, energy, business, space, education, religion, the judicial system, research, science . . . every field. They'll be our surgeons, our airline pilots, our judges, our national and international leaders, our educators, our spiritual mentors. With the right coaching, yours will be among them! Like I said, our world needs your kids!

These sometimes irascible adolescents will shape the future of our world during our lifetimes. What part will your son or your daughter have in that process? What destiny will they fulfill? What vision will they likely catch—from you?

You have no doubt helped change the world already. In large ways and small. But your greatest contribution will outlive you—your children and their children. You can help to shape the next generation and the generations that follow.

That's why some are willing to argue that the most important decision you ever made was to have kids. That is the rock you dropped in the pond whose ripples will extend beyond your imagination. That's why we are calling the principles we talk about here *Rare Kids; Well Done: Parenting Kids That Are Respectful, Responsible, and Obedient.* Because you and I and a generation of other parents are going to catch the vision and do what only moms and dads can. Now, that's pretty exciting stuff!

Do you know the name Norman Borlaug? I didn't either till I heard Andy Andrews tell his story.[4]

Norman Borlaug was born on his grandfather's farm near Cresco, Iowa, in 1914. The short story is that he became an agricultural scientist and changed the face of the globe. The *Wall Street Journal*

---

4   Andy Andrews, *The Butterfly Effect* (Thomas Nelson, 2010).

would call him "the man who fed the world." The story should include the fact that he was a champion wrestler in college and was inducted into the National Wrestling Hall of Fame in 1992. Also that he flunked his entrance exam when he attempted to enroll at the University of Minnesota.

Later he would be accepted and ultimately earn a Ph.D. in plant pathology and genetics. Borlaug would become one of his alma mater's most illustrious graduates and one of only six Americans ever to be awarded the Nobel Peace Prize, the Presidential Medal of Freedom, *and* the Congressional Gold Medal.

Dr. Borlaug developed strains of hybrid wheat and corn and other dwarf grains that could withstand abject growing conditions, including severe drought and poor soil. The studied consensus is that Norman Borlaug has been instrumental in saving from starvation the lives of more than a billion people (and counting) all over the earth. Borlaug was certainly a worthy recipient of the Nobel Peace Prize in 1970.

But don't go away; there's more to the story . . .

Borlaug began his groundbreaking research in one of the poorest sections of Mexico, sent there in 1944 by the United States government after officials had been urged on by the Rockefeller Foundation. The project found a ready ally in a man named Henry Wallace, the American vice president who served under Franklin Roosevelt. Wallace had been Secretary of Agriculture during Roosevelt's first term. He was a farmer by heritage and had done crop experimentation on his own, hybridizing high-yielding strains, especially of corn. Wallace was convinced that if used wisely, the planet had the capability of supporting its entire population.

From his position as vice president Wallace had the political clout to establish an agricultural experiment station in Mexico, and he sent Norman Borlaug there to head up the research on hybridizing grain crops. The resulting research Borlaug did changed the face of farming the world over and led to more than a billion people escaping the ravages of starvation. So it could perhaps be argued that Henry Wallace is the one who should have been awarded the Nobel Peace Prize.

But there's more yet to the story . . .

Where did Henry Wallace get his love for growing things and his belief that through careful management the land could be made more productive? How did Wallace become a champion of sturdy wheat?

When Henry was just a youngster—5 or 6 years old—his father became Professor of Dairy Sciences at the University of Iowa. A brilliant 19-year-old student named George enrolled in the biology department and took a liking to young Henry. Henry tagged along with the older student and from him learned to love every growing thing. On occasion Henry accompanied George and other students on excursions off campus to study how things grow. It was the beginning of a lifelong love affair between Henry Wallace and the things of nature, and would point Henry to a life that would eventually see him become U.S. Secretary of Agriculture under President Roosevelt.

So maybe it was that biology student named George – George Washington Carver – who should have received the Nobel Peace Prize.

But that's not the beginning of the story either . . .

Moses and Susan were farmers in Missouri. Although Missouri was a slave state, Moses and Susan did everything in their power to ease the suffering slavery created. They owned a slave family, but treated them like hired help. In fact, the slave mother, Mary and Susan became best friends.

Late one January night a band of hooligans, Quantrill's Raiders, came pillaging through the country, burned down Moses and Susan's barn, torched their crops, and killed several people. They kidnapped Mary, her 5-day-old son, and his 1-year-old sister.

The next morning Susan was so distraught that she appealed to Moses to do whatever he could to find Mary and the children. So Moses sent runners in all directions, finally made contact with Quantrill's Raiders, and arranged to meet them at a crossroads just over the state line in Kansas.

All through the night Moses rode his last remaining horse into western Kansas and met up with the ruffians. He learned that Mary and the young daughter were dead, but Moses agreed to swap his last horse for what they tossed to him in a dirty burlap bag.

As the hooded horsemen rode off into the night, Moses bent down and opened the bag. Inside was a baby boy, barely alive. Moses opened his coat and tucked the baby inside, keeping him alive by the warmth of his own body. All the rest of the night he walked, and as he walked he talked to the baby and sang to him. After Moses arrived home the next day, Moses and Susan decided that they would adopt the baby and raise him as their own. They would educate him, as they knew his mother would have wanted. And they would give him their name. So Mary's baby, whom she named George Washington, would grow up as George Washington Carver.

So maybe, in fact, the Nobel Peace Prize should have been awarded to two unassuming Missouri farmers, Moses and Susan Carver.

If any of those four people had been missing from that chain of events, the history of our world would have been measurably different. See, our world needs your kids. And it needs you to help get them to their intended destiny. Will it be to help save the planet from starvation? Who knows. Will it be to right grievous injustices? Who knows. Will it be to help restore honor to their generation? Who knows. Or will it be to teach a Sunday School class that changes young lives?

Will he be an honest painter who helps make a community more beautiful? Will she be a teacher who builds character as well as a grasp of the mysteries of calculus? Will he be an industrious fruit farmer who helps build a strong community as well as strong peach trees?

Will your daughter be a mom whose kids are an honor to the neighborhood, or your son become a dad whose conscience is not for sale? An athlete whose first loyalty is to purity, or an attorney who accepts a case only if it can be won with integrity?

Most of whatever they end up with they'll get from you.

One thing we know: There has never been another child just like yours. And there never will be. What splendid mark will he leave because you were his mom? What noble contribution will she make because you were her dad?

Our culture needs all of the honor and honesty, all of the judgment and justice, all of the love and laughter, all of the gratitude and graciousness, all of the respectfulness and responsibility it can get. Our world really needs your kids.

And remember: *Most of whatever they end up with they'll get from you.*

Are you up for the journey? Good; then let's move on.

CHAPTER 3

ME AND MY HEAVYWEIGHT COACH

For well over 50 years I've been watching the dynamics that go on in families. I've probably listened to stories from more parents and kids than you could get on a train. I've studied and analyzed and listened and read and prayed and consulted and observed and thought about how some families function well and others seem to be highly skilled in creating an adversarial environment . . . It seems they barely like one another.

I've watched more parent/teen teams go from friend to adversary, from adversary to friend, than you can imagine. Like you, I've seen a lot of teams where joy seems to reign supreme. I've also known the uneasy sense that all was not placid within my own clan. So let me describe the four ways I see families attempting to get from here to there.

1. HANDS ON

You've seen this kind of parenting—parents who insist on making all the decisions for their kids. Because Mom and Dad can do it better, Mom and Dad do it.

Being overprotected, these kids go through life believing that someone will always come to their rescue. And besides, they probably couldn't get it right themselves anyway. Because they don't get to make decisions or take responsibility for their outcomes, these kids often grow up having a hard time understanding one of life's most profound insights: *all behavior has consequences.* (It's going to seem like I keep harping on this consequences issue; you're right. It's a great teacher.)

They have a hard time managing their money. They have trouble getting places on time. Attempts to discipline them are often noisy but largely ineffective. They are not happy when they are expected to take responsibility for their behavior.

Recently I read that in some places in the Michigan elementary education system, there is no longer any such thing as a failing grade. That's ridiculous. Life is not fail-safe. Reality has a component called failure, and part of growing up is learning to deal with it. You can make a decision in an instant that will give you heartache for life. Those who learn that while they're young are blessed.

If your eighth-grader doesn't do her homework and gets a failing grade, Mom or Dad should not protest to the teacher. If your third-grader rides his bike recklessly and hits a tree, don't sue the landscaper for planting it there. If your teenage daughter gets pregnant before marriage, don't pretend it's the boy's fault. It takes two to tango.

My mom always told me that if I got a spanking at school, I'd get another one when I got home. I never put that thesis to the test, but I grew up believing she meant it.

The youngster who has a family member who is always there to step in front, place the blame on someone else, run interference, or make excuses is the youngster who will likely grow into adulthood responding like a victim to life, living with an entitlement mentality, and never understanding that he or she is not the center of the known universe.

2. HANDS OFF

You often read in the newspaper about kids from these kinds of families. They are the ones whose stories make you shake your head and ask, "How could a mere child do such a thing?" Part of the answer may lie in the fact that Mom and Dad are distracted, apparently disinterested, career-driven, selfish, preoccupied, overwhelmed, or all of the above.

I've occasionally asked these kinds of parents if they thought bringing a child into the world and on to responsible maturity could be accomplished on autopilot. Can you really just set them on cruise control and head off to work, hoping that some kind of celestial GPS will ultimately get them to the right destination? It generally doesn't set well when I ask that question.

Now, I don't want to amplify guilt in any parent or family that has to do heroics to provide financially for their children. I deeply respect parents who must struggle to keep the rent paid and food on the table. I grew up in a home like that.

Sometimes it takes major creativity to find a "clothes swap" in which parents do the hand-me-down thing outside of their own family. Or to organize a deal to do trade-off babysitting rather than pay a sitter. Or to find a vacant field where they can plant a garden. That is noble.

What I am describing are those family settings where, either physically or emotionally, the members of the family unit live separate lives. Dad sees his career as his number one priority. After all, if he doesn't nurture that, how can he provide for his family like they wish to be provided for? *That is an age-old cop-out.*

When our own two sons were growing up, I fought that every day of my life. As a clergyman I had been groomed to believe that I was supposed to have everyone else's welfare on my heart. After all, I was being paid to provide nurture to all of the hurting people in my parish. I was older than I should have been before I picked up on what I was doing. It took me a while to understand the principle from the Bible that goes like this (with some editing): "What shall it profit a man if he helps the whole neighborhood, but slights his own kids?" That's why I can describe this aberration with some accuracy and some conviction.

Or Mom, maybe with a career of her own, or simply a cluster of compelling interests outside her own home, leaves notes, parks the kids, gives instructions for fixing their own supper when they come home from school to an empty house, leaves a message on the answering machine saying that the sitter for tonight is named Sally, or otherwise communicates, "Hey, I'm sorry, but you are down my list of priorities quite a ways." That is a common enough phenomenon that we have coined a term to describe it: latchkey kids.

Kids who grow up in this environment often get much of their education from their peers, fear that no one is in their corner, don't develop a strong value system, and don't build a strong commitment to family loyalty.

3. HEAVY-HANDED

One of the cheapest ways to enforce conduct is if you have the authority—just because you can. A 5-foot-10-inch dad can raise his voice or his hand and get a 4-year-old to pick up his toys or else, but that's a shortcut to the kind of obedience a 4-year-old should be learning . . . or the way he should be learning to feel about his dad.

Children who learn to respond to an authoritarian (I'm not talking about *authoritative*—that's different; more later), demanding voice in their home tend to grow up alienated, resentful, and devious. The reason is quite simple: It is not easy to learn to respect someone who yells at you. That's why I'm clear on this simple principle: Never argue with your kids.

"Dr. Don, I don't think you just said what I think you just said. You're not being rational. You're suggesting I should *never* argue with my kids?"

Never.

"But you don't know my kids! I've got strong-headed teens!"

I don't have to know your strong-headed teens; I know the outcome, and it's not the one you're looking for.

"Explain that."

OK, here's the deal. When you argue with your kids, several things happen, none of which is taking you in the direction you want to go. First, you give up your authority as the parent. When you are matching argument for argument with an angry adolescent, you have come down to their level. Most teens love to see how many of your hot buttons they can push anyway, and an argument gives them a great practice field. Even though you may think you came out on top, you never win an argument with a teen.

See, you have just leveled the playing field, and it isn't supposed to be level. You are the adult here; you are the coach. You are the authority. You are, after all, the parent, and parents are to be obeyed, not debated. You are the leader, and leaders are to be followed, not confronted. I know, I know, not every family life authority agrees with me—and I respect their right to be wrong. But the fact is, parent-child governance is not a democracy. We'll have much more on this later; I'm just describing parenting styles here.

Also, a huge issue in family relations is respect—respect that goes both ways. Don't miss this: *A huge issue in family relations is respect. HUGE!* If a group of people—virtually any size and any relationship—have *profound respect* for one another, they can weather most any storm, learn to disagree agreeably, work through their differences, and come out the other end still liking one another.

But if you're in a shouting match, most of that isn't likely to happen. Further, you're sending a strong message that the way adults work out disagreements is to raise their voices; thus you end up perpetuating nonproductive conflict into another generation.

"OK, so I have just decided that I won't argue with my kids. That's a great idea, but how do I make it work in my house?" Thanks for asking. We're going to spend a fair amount of time in the pages ahead getting really specific about this issue because it is so basic to "Rare Kids; Well Done" parenting.

In the meantime, here's a summary of the "no arguing" principles:

FIVE REASONS NEVER TO ARGUE WITH YOUR KIDS . . .

1. When you argue, you've already lost the battle, because you have allowed your kids to successfully level the playing field. You are no longer in control but are being forced to use the same tools *they* are using. It erodes the healthy authority structure in a family. The fact is, you are not your child's roommate or buddy— you are the parent.

2. It is bad modeling. Kids need to learn that there are more productive ways to work through disagreements than each one trying to outshout the other. Healthy people who respect each other don't settle issues on the basis of who can verbally outmaneuver the other.

3. It creates/demonstrates an atmosphere of mutual disrespect. People who care deeply about each other—as is generally true in healthy families—weigh their words so as not to offend; this is a lesson that needs to be learned in the family so that it spills over into all relationships.

4. It sets up a win/lose dynamic. You either *win* an argument or you *lose* an argument. Healthy relationships always seek for an outcome in which there are no losers.

5. It is often emotionally damaging because it is not uncommon for words to be spoken and feelings expressed in the heat of a shouting match that carry long-term hurt.

WHAT TO DO INSTEAD . . .

1. Listen. Assume the best. Do not criticize or judge. If you listen to your kids when they're 9, they'll still talk to you when they're 16.

2. Do not allow yourself to be drawn into an argument. If the air is charged, just say, "We'll have this discussion when the atmosphere is a little more placid."

3. Insist that one of the rules of a happy family is respect. If you violate that rule, it will cost you privileges.

4. If a discussion begins to get heated, walk away. "I don't want to process this now; we'll talk later."

5. Before you allow yourself to be drawn into a sparring match, remind yourself of your goals for your family. Ask yourself: Is what I am about to say going to contribute to my vision and my goals for my kids? Will it inspire? Will it be taking the high road? Will it motivate and encourage? Will it help build feelings of self-worth and value in them?

6. Remember that everything you say produces an effect in the one who hears it. It changes them. That being so, it is awesome to realize that your words have creative power . . . power to make change. What kind of change will be created by the words you are about to say? Do they fit with your goals?

4. COACH

Maybe I like the word coach because I've had some really good coaches.

When I was, I think, 11, my mother (we were a single-parent family from the time I was 6 till about 12) unilaterally decided that I was going to learn to play the violin.

"Aw, come on, Mom, none of my friends play the violin. How can I play in the Boone Avenue Bunglers [the neighborhood jazz band all of us vied to be in—we lived on Boone Avenue in Spokane, Washington] with a violin? How about the trumpet? Or sax?"

Nope; I didn't even get a vote.

As it turned out, Mr. Harris was a very capable—if corpulent—music coach. I came to his class with below-zero violin aptitude and even less enthusiasm. Three years later I was playing in the Spokane All-City Youth Ensemble. True, it wasn't the Boone Avenue Bunglers, but it was quite a thrill, and I probably learned more.

Mr. Harris inspired me and encouraged me. He helped me discover the thrill of great music. He pushed our whole string section and stretched us to do things we didn't dream we could do. He drilled us relentlessly on the basics. He didn't demand perfection, only excellence. We played music we had heard only on records (records!) we couldn't afford to buy. He had people standing on their feet cheering when they heard us. How great is that for a kid from a broken home?

You can see why I like the term coach.

So let's talk about a parent type that functions as a coach. As with sports, a parent-coach brings out the best qualities in the team.

- A wise coach has deep respect for every player.

- A smart coach helps the individuals on the team develop skills, including decision-making skills.

- An effective coach sits players on the bench when that is the most appropriate decision. Pulling rank is available when needed. A good coach is a leader and is not derailed even if a player disagrees or doesn't understand.

- A savvy coach builds team loyalty, knowing that nobody gets where they need to go by themselves. You've heard the story about the turtle on the fence post. If you ever see one, you know one fact for sure: it didn't get there by itself.

- A caring coach is an encourager who talks the team through those times when they don't perform well, all the while continuing to insist that all players follow the game plan and give their best.

- An effective coach discusses options for "next time" rather than emphasizing blame.

- A winning coach who builds for the future searches out the strengths of those on the team and builds on those skills, maybe even strengths the team members didn't see in themselves.

Lay those seven coaching protocols over against your parenting practices and see how you measure up.

I know you're thinking, "You know, that 'coach' term is looking better all the time; it's a pretty uncanny metaphor for a parent . . . I'd like to explore what that might look like for my role in our family. How do we get there from here?"

OK, I'm ready if you are. Next chapter, please.

REPROGRAMMING THE KING

You: The Resident Valet

BIRTH – 24 MONTHS

From the moment her new son graces earth with his presence, Mom moves from host to valet. Definition: "Valet: an attendant [for instance, in a hotel] who performs personal services for customers." And you will doubtless remember the adage "The customer is *king!*"

There are some interesting parallels . . .

The slightest noise from the throne, and the servant rushes to his majesty's side, day or night. Every need is tended to—anticipated even—and none is too small or too nasty. His majesty is napping—the house must be quiet. Unplug the phone. Speak in hushed tones. He requires special clothing and special food. His schedule rules the family. The bathwater must be a perfect temperature. Put the unthinkable in the washing machine. Special shampoos are acquired that do not sting his sensitive eyes.

This is the stuff accorded royalty.

And then there is travel—ah, travel. Off for a weekend to Grandma's house . . . Dad takes an overnight case (small). Mom takes an overnight case (small) plus a pair of wrinkled jeans and a loose-fitting blouse.

The king, on the other hand, has boxes and bottles and bags and nutritional supplements and even special transportation devices. That was a wise decision to upgrade to an SUV. It also makes you wonder what it would be like if Grandma lived more than three houses away.

A trip to the mall further establishes his domain. He is wheeled about in an elaborate mobile throne. Subjects, even strangers, bow before him and are enchanted. Should his majesty favor them with a smile or a gurgle, they swoon with glee and come rushing from all directions with camera phones.

And Dad . . . Where is he in all this? Dad is the valet-in-training. He is the apprentice, the backup. He spends most of the game on the bench. He is sent in if the valet is injured.

He doesn't know the protocols. He doesn't get it. The way we know he doesn't get it is because when the valet must be away even for a short time, she will leave him lists—and instructions—and phone numbers.

At no other time in his life will this youngster flourish while being micromanaged.

Why all this fuss? Ah, we must keep his majesty happy.

Question: Is all this bad or good? Necessary or unnecessary?

Easy answer: It is essential. It is a necessity. It is imperative. It is not an option. The child is totally dependent on others. At no other time in his life will this youngster flourish while being micromanaged—having every decision made for him and every need instantly met. But at this time in his life it is his only means of surviving. Mom and Dad acknowledged that a few months ago when they signed on for the role of valets, and there is no backing out now.

If by some huge good fortune Grandma does indeed live nearby, there may be occasional brief interludes; otherwise this role goes well beyond that of the valet, who goes home at the end of the shift; it comes closer to that of an indentured servant.

I am not concerned whether you, Mom and Dad, will do well in this role. Those who pick up a book like this one are not the parents who worry me. But let me leverage just a bit more the significance of these first 24 months.

The king is learning more than we are intentionally teaching.

The king is learning more than we are intentionally teaching. By the very way he is handled he comes to understand what love feels like. By the way he is talked to and sung to and made to giggle, he is beginning to sense what it feels like to be cared for. Though it will be a long time before he can put it into words, he has already begun to experience feelings that will shape acceptance and security in his life.

You thought that "this-little-piggy-went-to-market" business on his toes was maybe a waste of time? It wasn't.

Your touch will become his refuge. Your warmth will be his comfort. Your lullaby will be his peace. Some call it bonding; I call it love. The first word he will ever say will probably be your name. It will be one of the happiest days of your life.

2 – 3 YEARS

One night, quite unsuspecting, you tuck in Prince Charming, and the next morning Ivan the Terrible awakens.

Did you see that bend in the road approaching probably about two years into the journey?[5]

One night, quite unsuspecting, you tuck in Prince Charming, and the next morning Ivan the Terrible awakens. His world is beginning to change, and he doesn't like it. All he has ever known is wall-to-wall service, and now it seems the wait staff is going on strike. No one jumps when he beckons. And the expectations begin to accumulate. Mom insists he learn to feed himself. When nature calls he must stop whatever he is doing and go sit on a cold, hard seat with a hole in it. Often during the day he is expected to follow instructions.

The typical reaction from his majesty is not pretty. We even have a name for it—*the terrible twos*. It appears to the king that his personal valet is working off of a new job description. There has been a mutiny in the ranks of the faithful. The crown he has worn without question all his life is being snatched from his head by irresponsible staff members.

Experience has taught him that the only way to deal with incompetence is with anger. If he is not served, someone will pay. Tantrum time.

Yup, the terrible twos.

---

5   Kids this age don't read calendars much, so the time periods are approximate.

In case anyone should ask you, tell them I said that's a really stupid idea.

What Sir Fuss-a-lot doesn't realize is that he is entering what is perhaps the most important transition period of his life. He must learn that he is not the center of the universe after all. The people he encounters are not there to serve him after all. Tantrums are attempted power grabs, and he must learn that they don't work after all.

So what are a mom and dad to do? Not nothing. Not ignore it; it won't go away. Not respond with some kind of aggressive punishment. Not give in to it; not ever. Recently I read one "authority" who says, "If your child pitches a tantrum in public and is on the floor wailing and flailing, you should get down on the floor with her, rub her back, and quietly try to talk her through the tantrum." In case anyone should ask you, tell them I said that's a really stupid idea.

What, then?

Here's a possibility that works with many kids. Select a room—a spare bedroom or preferably a bathroom. This becomes the "get happy room." No parental shouting; no threats; no pleading. Just leadership. The child is told, "This is the place where you can holler and cry and fuss as long as you want. You can go to the potty when you need to and get a drink of water when you need to. When you're happy again, you can come out." Trust me, it won't take long.

See, not having an audience takes the theater out of the tantrum. And tantrums are about theater. Now no one is watching this staged emotional meltdown, and since it's obvious no one is being moved by it, its effectiveness is neutered. Remember the old question "If a tree falls in the forest and no one is there to hear it, does it still make a sound?" Here's how I'd ask that question: "If a child stages a tantrum and no one is there to watch it, does it accomplish its purpose?" The answer to the first question is yes. The answer to the second question is no.

The default position of human nature is selfishness.

Back to Sir Fuss-a-lot . . . The default position of human nature is selfishness. We all instinctively want our own way. Left to itself, that heart condition does not heal. That's why the epoch between the second and third birthdays is so pivotal in the life of a child, because the mind-set must move from "Look, everyone, I have my own personal full-time valet!" to "Whoa, now they're expecting me to pay attention when they talk to me."

The problem is, kids are *going to school* still not having made this transition. Those kinds of kids age teachers. They wring the fun out of teaching. These are the kids who have never learned to cooperate. They don't know the deep joy of a job well done. They have yet to experience the satisfaction of self-discipline. They don't focus. They stare out the window. They punch other kids in line. They don't get their work done on time. They are disrespectful of teachers and peers alike. In many schools, as bizarre as this sounds, they will receive a diagnosis with a lot of capital letters in it—and a bottle of pills.[6]

This whole transition process is crucial enough that where there are two parents, they will want to work at it together. Kids do best when they're double-teamed. But by the very nature of the assignment, Mom will usually carry the major role. Here's a checklist for at least three of the tasks that are hers during this third year.

1. She must begin working toward having the child carry all the responsibilities of which he/she is capable. Let me be even stronger with that. She must begin not doing for the child anything the child can do for himself. He can help set the table. He can—with assistance at first—learn to make his own bed. He can get his own drink of water if there is a glass and stool in easy reach. He can put his dirty clothes in the laundry. He can pick up his toys. He can brush his own teeth. He can bring the storybook at bedtime.

6   I feel very keenly about this travesty. For a full discussion of this fairly recent phenomenon, see the book by my friend and colleague, John Rosemond, entitled *The Diseasing of America's Children*, written with Bose Ravenel, M.D.

It's called reality. They will not be waited on hand and foot the rest of their lives. Now is the time this awareness needs to awaken. In fact, an ennobling character quality we will want to be grooming early is one of service. The next step will be to guide them to look for ways they can be helpful to others, but for right now, the key lesson is "You can do that, honey. I will help you learn how." Confidence comes from successes, and in this setting there are many.

2. Mom (especially) must begin to establish boundaries with her child.

I find it fascinating that the bookstores are filled with books about all kinds of people-boundaries. Boundaries with your siblings; boundaries with your ex; boundaries with your boss; boundaries with your date; even boundaries with your husband. But hardly anybody is writing much about establishing boundaries with your kids. Seems like kind of a forbidden topic.

The reason for that may be partly because it sounds selfish. Almost heartless. The fact is, the boundaries you establish with your kids are as much for their benefit as for yours. When you build the right kinds of limits, everybody wins.

That little ankle-biter (a favorite Kevin Leman term) is needing to become a stand-alone. He/she must move from the confining world of total dependence into the freedom of self-determination. Till now he has depended on you for everything, often even the very sustenance of life. But he was not born to walk in your shadow. He is destined to cut his own swath, and one of your major duties right now is to help him begin to learn how to use his own sickle.

So, what's that going to look like? For one thing it means that Mom is going to begin to paint a different picture of herself to her child than the child has ever had before. The child will look for but not find the sign Mom has worn around her neck for the past couple of years that said, "I am your Mom; give me my instructions." At a parenting seminar in North Carolina one mom reported that her neighbor had recently told her, "My goal is to make every day of my son's life the happiest day of his life." I'm sorry; that's not good preparation for life.

Reprogramming the King

There are still basic needs to be met, of course; that won't go away for several years, but the mood changes. For more than two years Mom has fixated on the child. Every sniffle. Every whimper. Every desire. You can almost count on your fingers the daylight minutes that little one has been out of Mom's sight except to nap. But there is a sea change here, and Miss Prissy moves from captain to buck private, from senior in one school to freshman in the next. Mom and Dad's emphasis moves from being sustainers to leaders.

Leadership. Let's talk about leadership. Leaders chart the course and keep the troops on task. People look up to good leaders. Leaders have a vision not shared by the led because they have the long view in mind. The led don't always enjoy the decisions made by the leaders, but leadership is not about popularity; that's politics. Leadership is about establishing goals that will result in the most desirable outcomes for the led and then moving intentionally and relentlessly toward them.

There was a bunch of philosophy in that last paragraph; let's talk about your 3-year-old . . .

In the grand design of the universe it has been determined that little kids need leaders, albeit loving leaders. It takes a couple of years to get past the fragile state to when learning can begin in earnest. Now little Egbert is having experiences that move him along toward independence.

Autonomy isn't a word I use a lot, do you? It's a helpful word, though. In our setting it means that the child is beginning to become a Me. He is beginning to unhook from the big people in his life and become a self-governing human being. Mom (and Dad) will work to see that that happens. They will still read to him (hopefully at least a half hour a day at this age), and they will still play with him (though not necessarily on demand and not for long periods). They will still provide for his physical care. They will still love on him at every opportunity. But the movement will be toward helping him become independent. By the time he is 3, he should be able to play alone for an hour or more.

"An hour? Wow. My 3-year-old gets bored with his toys in five minutes."

Really? H'mmm. What kinds of toys?

Well, really caring parents buy their kids lots of really neat toys, right?

It depends on your definition of "really neat toys." Let's talk about toys for a minute. Most toys are single-purpose. A shiny plastic airplane will probably always be a shiny plastic airplane. A windup dog that walks and barks will probably always be a windup dog that walks and barks. There are only so many things you can do with a shiny plastic airplane and a windup dog that walks and barks. But consider some other options.

A little pile of blocks (consider no more than five or six at a time at this age) can be a lot of things. Think of all the things you could do with the center core from a roll of paper towels. It could be a megaphone, a drumstick, a big wheel, a long nose, a telescope, a trumpet, a bat, a rocket, a bowling pin to knock down with a ball, a boat . . . Your 2½-year-old can come up with more ideas than I can. A couple of empty thread spools (remember those?), play dough, puppets, some small boxes, a mixing spoon, a paper sack, a plastic bowl (doubles as a hat), a blanket (add a couple of chairs and it makes a great tent), a picture book. The list goes on. But not too many all at once. A dozen is probably too many. Cheap. Creativity-enhancers. Autonomy-builders.

That means Mom gets a little more quiet time, too, and that's an important bonus.

OK, little Egbert is learning to do things for himself—and others. He is discovering that he is his own person and Mom does not appear every time he rings the bell. He is not permitted to sleep in the marriage bed. Signs of independence begin to appear.

Here's agenda item **#3** for Mom, and it's a dandy.

As the second year of the toddler's life progresses, Mom and Dad get to redevelop their own relationship. The realities of birthing and rearing an infant have been demanding beyond what either of them anticipated. For more than two years they have invested virtually every ounce of emotional and physical energy they could summon in the child. Now it's time for them to reinvest in each other.

Back to date nights again. Regularly. In fact, they will now begin to invest more time and emotion in each other than they do in the child. Why? Because the most important thing parents can do for their children is to love each other. The most essential thing you can do for your kids, Dad, is to love their mom. The security and serenity that are part of every healthy baby's rightful heritage grow out of being in the presence of a mom and dad who clearly are very much in love with each other.

Obviously I'm not advocating neglect. What I am suggesting is a course of action designed to correct a grievous imbalance that has swept across the land. Let me describe it.

In much of Mommyland, USA, the protocol says that the more time and emotion parents (especially moms) invest in their kids, the better parents they are. Thus the rush to enroll 3-year-olds in swimming classes; to teach them, not only their numbers and the alphabet and all the colors in the box, but also all the state capitals. Now watch this because it is omnipresent: *The toddler's accomplishments become the measure of the mother.* In no generation before ours have mothers felt more pressure from other mothers to do such heroics for their children.

But remember our definition of leadership. A leader is one who looks down the road, establishes a goal, and moves inexorably toward it. Let me tell you what parents have taught me. I love to ask a group of moms and dads in a place where I'm speaking to look ahead to the time their kids will leave home and marry . . . maybe 15 or 20 years into the future. I ask them to list *five of the most important traits* they want their kids to have.

Without exception the lists will include words such as "honest, compassionate, unselfish, caring, thoughtful, industrious, dependable." Almost never will words show up such as "wealthy, influential, married to the prom queen, high IQ, well-coordinated, clever, graduate of a prestigious university." That being true then, wise leadership is going to zero in on those traits in the first sentence above and build an environment in which they are nurtured.

That is a liberating insight. In many households the term "stay-at-home mom" is a cruel joke. Early on she becomes a "drive-around mom" and only exchanges crib-side servitude for curbside servitude. Egbert must be moved out of his role as the hub around which the family revolves; that position belongs to Dad and Mom. Reenter romance.

We are setting the stage here for some big issues. Outcomes from our "terrible twos strategy" will impact the lad's self-confidence, his creativity, his attitude toward others—especially toward females— his respect for others, his respect for authority, his entitlement expectations, his feelings of self-worth, whether he will be self-reliant, self-centered, thoughtful. Interesting; it looks a lot like that list of qualities Mom and Dad say they are looking for in their children. This 20- to 36-month era in my child's growing up is looking pretty significant . . pretty foundational. I'd better get it right.*

---

* I am indebted to John Rosemond for many of the insights in this chapter.

MOM, DAD, MEET THE DENDRITES

I wish I could tell you how important it is that your kids not watch television.

"At what age, Dr. Don?"

"Well, certainly not as infants, toddlers, or young children."

"You mean, maybe not a lot till they're 5?"

"No, I mean probably not much till they're 12."

I use the TV as a babysitter for my toddler? That thing is a lifesaver!

"Twelve? You're kidding, right? Do you know how that would mess up my afternoon quiet time and meal preparation, which is when I use the TV as a babysitter for my toddler? That thing is a lifesaver!"

Actually, I'm *not* kidding, even though there is not unanimity among the experts as to when it is "safe" to expose youngsters to the electronic screen. My attitude on issues like this is always "Let's take the safe route." So I say 12. I know it's going to mess up a lot of people's schedules and put me on the "Most Wanted" list of a lot of kids, but let me share some of the compelling reasons.

This may surprise you as much as it did me, but did you know that 68 percent of all children age 2 (!) and under will watch TV or a video on a typical day in America? And they will watch for an average of more than two hours. Every day.

A fourth (26 percent) of America's 2-and-unders have a TV in their bedroom, which they can watch from their crib[7] (giving birth, I suppose, to a new term: crib potato).

A landmark study done in 2003 at the Child Health Institute at Children's Hospital and Regional Medical Center in Seattle, Washington, led by its director, Dr. Dimitri Christakis, caused the pediatric community to take a new look at the influence of the electronic screen on very young children.

---

[7] These statistics are from a study done by the Henry J. Kaiser Family Foundation and the Children's Digital Media Center (CDMC) in 2003, so we've known this stuff for a long time.

The study involved more than 2,500 children, 1 year old and 3. One of the very telling conclusions of the study was this: "Early television exposure is associated with attentional (that is, the ability to pay attention) problems at age 7." In summary, Dr. Christakis, a Seattle pediatrician, found that children who watched television as babies are more likely to have shorter attention spans, problems concentrating, and impulsiveness.

I find that very informative, because the current majority opinion in the mental health community is that the "attentional" types of problems—think ADD (attention deficit disorder)—are genetic, that is to say, hereditary. Thus, the treatment protocol of choice is to medicate—give 'em a pill (even though it's clear that pills don't "rewire" the brain; the symptoms will probably return within six to 12 months).

But now we learn that attention problems at 7—a common time for them to show up in school—may be linked to what was happening in the child's brain after he was born, but before he was even old enough to sit up.

The research outcomes continue to mount. A 2005 University of Pennsylvania study found that watching *Sesame Street* before age 3 actually delayed a child's ability to develop language skills. This may be because babies are wired to be active and not passive learners.

His developing brain is being assaulted by long periods of unnaturally short bursts of visual stimulation.

At these early ages *program content* seems to be practically irrelevant. The issue is not that the child is watching an objectionable program, but that his developing brain is being assaulted by long periods of unnaturally short bursts of visual stimulation. As frequently as every 3.5 seconds on average in some programming, the camera cuts to a new scene, a new perspective, a new angle, a new character, a new activity. The wiring that is developing in the dendrite portion of the baby's brain is being taught to function with a micro attention span, which, when he gets to school, is apt to make it seem as though this first-grader is high on caffeine.

In 1998 the American Academy of Pediatrics handed down the recommendation that their 55,000 physicians should counsel parents not to allow children to watch *any* television before the age of 2. None.

Still, babies are glued to television sets, with 40 percent of 3-month-olds and nearly 90 percent of those 3 and under regularly watching TV, according to a University of Washington study released in July 2007. These tiny viewers are further proof that baby TV is a booming business. Today, infants have their own 24-hour network (which one British organization—Whitespot.com—calls "the first 24-hour infomercial for attention deficit disorder"), Brainy Baby and Baby Einstein DVDs, and a growing list of other programs made just for them. Baby Einstein-type DVDs have had sales of more than $500,000,000.[8]

This is essential information for anyone who has kids, wants kids, or even likes kids.

In a study published in the *Journal of Pediatrics* in August 2007, researchers found that, among babies ages 8 months to 16 months, every hour spent daily watching programs such as Brainy Baby or Baby Einstein actually translated into six to eight *fewer* words in their vocabularies as compared with other children their age. Face it, TV is a lousy substitute for mom.

Yale University television researcher Dorothy Singer observes, "When one-year-olds are playing with a toy, they can explore it, poke at it, drop it. They're learning about space, about sound, and they're developing a sense of competence. Watching a TV show just doesn't provide the same sensory experience."

---

8   In 2001 Walt Disney bought the company, founded by Julie Aigner-Clark of Denver, but by 2007 Disney was offering refunds to any parent who was concerned that the DVDs would be harmful to the mental development of their child.

On March 4, 2009, CNNHealth.com reported: "Based on the existing body of research, [Dr. Marie Evans] Schmidt, a developmental psychology instructor at Harvard Medical School, said, 'There's still *more evidence of harm than benefit* as far as TV viewing in infancy is concerned.'"

And American researchers are not the only ones to discover the potential damage caused by early TV for youngsters. In 2008 France's broadcast authority banned French channels from airing TV shows aimed at children under 3 years old. The High Audiovisual Council of France pointed out:

> Television viewing hurts the development of children under three years old and poses a certain number of risks, encouraging passivity, slow language acquisition, over-excitedness, troubles with sleep and concentration, as well as dependence on [electronic] screens.

I know; some of this is technical stuff, and cute stories make for more interesting reading, but this is essential information for anyone who has kids, wants kids, or even likes kids.

A diagnosis such as ADD (or ADHD, Attention Deficit Hyperactivity Disorder) is just one of the issues that leave many teachers—and many parents—stressed. Ongoing research indicates that there are other neurological issues that may likely be triggered by television.

For instance, in 2005 the research team of Waldman, Nicholson, and Adilov from Cornell University studied the relationship between early television viewing and autism. In conclusion they observed:

> As a final point, although as discussed our results do not definitively prove that early childhood television watching is an important trigger for autism, we believe our results provide sufficient support for the possibility that until further research can be conducted it might be prudent to act as if it were.

"Prudent to act as if it were . . ." Wise counsel, since ongoing research continues to provide evidence of the fact that the incidence of erratic childhood behavior and lowered academic performance have virtually paralleled the penetration of television into America's homes. As the presence of television has grown, so have the symptoms of its ill effects.

We've been talking about preschoolers, infants, and the under 3's, but earlier I said that television is a factor in the development of kids much later than 3 as well. Let me tell you what we know about that, and then I want to make some suggestions as to how leadership parents can decide what to do with the often unwelcome intrusion of TV into their home and family.

What does television viewing do to kids as they move toward and through the elementary grades? Short answer: It affects every facet of life of those who are "heavy" (code word for "watches a lot") TV viewers. Time. Health. Social skills. Family dynamics. Spare time options (think hobbies, sports, music, reading, exercise, fresh air, thinking). Academics. Vocabulary growth.

America's typical pre-teen will watch more than 8,000 hours of television by the time she finishes sixth grade.

And no wonder; that's where America's kids live—TVville. It's pervasive. It's intrusive. The elephant in the den. The 800-pound gorilla. America's typical pre-teen will watch more than 8,000 hours of television by the time she finishes sixth grade. That's more time than she'll spend on any other single activity she has done in her waking hours. In fact, it's 1,600 more hours than she will have spent in school. Sixteen hundred hours is forty 40-hour weeks!

But that's not all. Those issues listed above—time, health, academics, etc.—are just the obvious casualties. As a child passes 5 and moves toward the classroom, there is a dramatic change in how his/her brain processes information, so the toll television exacts of a

12-year-old is much different from that of a 2-month old. The major change is that now program content also begins to become a huge factor. Not the only factor, but huge nonetheless.

It was Dallas Cowboys' coaching legend Tom Landry who said,

"Leadership is getting someone to do what they don't want to do, to achieve what they want to achieve."

That is one of the most profound descriptions of leadership—on or off the football field—that I have ever heard.

If I could encapsulate what I want to say in the next few pages, it would read just about like that. Leaders—leadership parents—have a vision, a goal. Leadership parents look ahead; they are not content to be steering by the clouds. Leadership parents are driven by a dream and often make difficult, unpopular decisions to accomplish long-term goals.

Let me list three goals that seem to me to be crucial to the dreams of leadership parents and their management of the screen:

GOAL #1:
I WANT MY KIDS TO BECOME AVID AND ARDENT READERS.

Remember RIF—Reading Is Fundamental? It was established in 1966 to encourage children to read, and to date RIF has provided more than 325,000,000 free books to some of our nation's most under-resourced kids. Why? Because, among other benefits, reading develops language skills, and that is at the heart of education, communication, understanding, success, and survival in our culture.

I want my children to learn to read, but more, I want my children to learn to *love* to read. And the love for reading comes from reading. And from being read to. *All the research shows that the more kids watch TV, the less they read.*

Reading is hard work. There is something mentally taxing about translating inanimate objects such as letters into letter groups that have meaning, that paint pictures, that tell stories. It's easier to look at pictures as they pass by on the screen, because that can be done in a totally passive mental state. But to read or be read to requires a focus that is essential to jump-start the expansion of a child's mind. TV is easier; reading is better.

I remember when, in 1958, the International Paper Company began running a series of classic print ads with the tagline: "Send me a man who reads." (Today it would be worded "Send me a *person* who reads.") The premise of the ad was that people who read are more effective and more successful, driving results in organizations.

At the time it didn't seem that a campaign like that was needed. Reading in the U.S. was on a roll. Book sales increased by 447 percent between 1940 and 1960, during which time the population increased only 37 percent.

Today, things look different. Books sales have been flat for a decade. An Associated Press-Ipsos poll in 2007 found that a quarter of Americans had not read a book during the preceding year. Let me introduce you to a term that educators use: reluctant reader. It seems as though there's quite a bit of that going around. I'm convinced that we can place much of the blame for that reality on the shoulders of America's television addiction.

Now remember, leadership parents take the long look. They forego immediate pleasures for long-term goals; they work at "getting someone to do what they don't want to do, to achieve what they want to achieve." You can see further than your kids can see; your goal is to help them see that the magnificence of the goal is worth any temporary discomfort of the journey. Kids who read go further than kids who don't. Television keeps them from it.

GOAL #2:
I WANT MY KIDS TO BE COMPASSIONATE, UNSELFISH, CARING CITIZENS.

Literally *thousands* of studies since the 1950s have explored whether there is a link between exposure to media violence and violent behavior. All but 18 of those studies have answered "yes."

The evidence from the research is overwhelming. According to the American Academy of Pediatrics, "Extensive research evidence indicates that media violence can contribute to aggressive behavior, desensitization to violence, nightmares, and fear of being harmed."[9]

Two-thirds of all television programming includes violence, and the percentage is higher among children's programs than adult programs.[10] In a study reported in the *Journal of the American Medical Association,* every single animated feature film produced between 1937 and 1999 in America contained violence.[11]

Many shows actually glamorize violence, and TV often promotes violent acts as an effective way to get what you want, without consequences. Even "good guys" beating up "bad guys" gives a message that violence is normal and OK. Many children will try to be like their "good guy" heroes in their play.

You and I have watched children play enough to know that they often imitate the violence they see on TV. Enough research has been done to know that repeated exposure to TV violence makes children less sensitive toward its effects on others and the human suffering it causes. Viewing violence on television leads to more aggressive behavior.

Enter Mom and Dad, whose fervent desire is to rear children who are "compassionate, unselfish, and caring." With our kids watching

---

9   American Academy of Pediatrics, Committee on Public Education. "Media Violence," *Pediatrics,* Vol. 108, No. 5, November 5, 2001, pp. 1222-6. Available at: http://aappolicy.aappublications.org/cgi/content/full/pediatrics;108/5/1222.

10   J. Federman, ed. National Television Violence Study. Vol 3 (Thousand Oaks, CA: Sage; 1998).

11   F. Yokota and K. M. Thompson, "Violence in G-rated Animated Films," *JAMA,* May 24, 2000, pp. 284, 285.

that much of the kind of television we've just described, it appears that Mom and Dad are swimming upstream in a fast river.

Here is an interesting exercise: Sit down with your spouse and compile a list of those character qualities you would like to see planted and nurtured in your youngster's heart. Your list will be different from anyone else's, but it will probably include some terms such as thoughtful, unselfish, courteous, kind, helpful, generous, forgiving. Now lay your list over against tonight's television schedule and decide whether your TV practices are helping or hindering the long-range goals you have in your heart for your family. My mother used to say, "Is it helpin' ya or ain't it?" Great question.

GOAL #3:
I WANT MY KIDS TO DEVELOP PURE CHARACTERS IN A DECAYING CULTURE.

I think Alexander Pope, the brilliant 18th-century English essayist and poet, maybe had it right when he wrote:

> Vice is a monster of so frightful mien,
>   As to be hated need but to be seen;
> Yet seen too oft, familiar with her face,
>   We first endure, then pity, then embrace.

I think he had it right, because we're watching the process at work. Sexually explicit programming that would have mortified (and enraged) the past generation is common fare in this one.

The number of sex scenes on TV has nearly doubled since 1998, with 70 percent of the top 20 most-watched shows by teens including sexual content.[12] Fifteen percent of scenes with sexual intercourse depict characters who have just met having sex. Of the shows with sexual content, an average of five scenes per hour involve sex.

---

12   D. Kunkel, K. Eyal, K. Finnerty, E. Biely, and E. Donnerstein, "Sex on TV," Kaiser Family Foundation, November 2005.

Watching sex on TV increases the chances a teen will have sex, and research suggests it may cause teens to start having sex at younger ages. Even viewing shows with characters *talking about sex* increases the likelihood of sexual initiation.[13] My friend Andy Andrews says, "It's hard to win against an enemy that has a fort in your head."

Let me just share my heart with you for a minute. Intimacy between a husband and wife has to be one of the most unique and precious gifts ever given to the human family. To cheapen it by promiscuous disregard of its meaning is to desecrate its sanctity and steal from it that which can never be replaced. Married sex, for many, loses its mystery and becomes boring when the partners have already discharged its magic in meaningless settings. Any influence— television included—that erodes its exclusiveness is a destructive force in that culture. Looking back over the history of nations, none has ever long survived whose morals collapsed in debauchery. Put that sword to the throat of your *TV Guide.*

And place the moral content of today's television alongside the passion in your heart as described in goal #3.

When I began writing this chapter I thought we'd work on maybe a half dozen goals, but on reflection perhaps three is enough to make the point. I want to offer some suggestions, because I know that many who read these pages will wrestle with the real world of changing a process that is deeply entrenched in their family's psyche. You may be one who is anticipating that suggesting dramatic changes in your family's television habits may create a little violence of its own.

Here are 17 ideas for managing TV-watching in your family. You won't find them all useful or even desirable. But hopefully you'll find one or several that will be. Feel free to mix and match:

1. If you elect to have television in your home, carefully consider the best place for it. When your children are small, use the old

---

13   R. L. Collins, M. N. Elliott, S. H. Berry, D. E. Kanouse, D. Kunkel, S. B. Hunter, and
    A. Miu, "Watching Sex on Television Predicts Adolescent Initiation of Sexual Behavior,
    Pediatrics, Sept. 2004, pp. 280-9.

adage "out of sight, out of mind," and keep the TV in a room away from where your family spends most of its time. As your kids get older, you might want it to be in a more visible place for easier monitoring. Note: Never put a television in a child's bedroom! Never.

2. If your kids aren't already too old, start young. It's wise to work on developing good TV-viewing habits well before your children start school. As they grow older, it will become more difficult for you to enforce restrictions or influence their tastes.

3. Kids model their behavior after that of their parents—so take a hard look at your own viewing habits, and if necessary, change them.

4. Don't leave your TV on when you're not watching it. Turn it on for a specific program, and turn it off again when the show is over. This makes television a special experience that your children can look forward to.

5. Consider a non-school-night rule. No TV on weeknights.

6. Try going without television for a few days to help you reevaluate the role it plays in your family's life. You can also join thousands of others and give up TV for a week during the annual TV Turnoff Week event.

7. Consider going "cold turkey." (I'm not sure where that term came from.) Many cities have no-smoking rules for all public buildings. Consider becoming a TV-free home.

8. Tell the parents of your children's friends about your television rules. It's difficult to control what your children see at other houses, but if parents talk about their TV rules with others, it's easier to protect children from unsuitable programming.

9. Encourage your children to watch a variety of programs: sports, nature, science, the arts, music, and history, for instance. There's a lot of great TV programming available that makes learning about the world interesting and fun. Help expand their TV horizon.

10. Remove the television from the area where your family eats its meals. There may be no better way to jeopardize family time together than to have a TV set attempting to join the conversation from the corner.

11. Each week look over the program schedule and decide which programs your family will watch. Limit viewing time to those preselected times.

12. When your children are of appropriate age, discuss the values your family holds, and explain how your television choices are affected by those values. It is a leadership parent's goal that the children become increasingly self-directed in their television choices.

13. Have fun with your new goals. Admit your own struggles. Lighten up as you seek to build some new disciplines into your family's viewing habits.

14. Seek to entice your children to broaden their interests. The Parents as Teachers National Center says that young children need to "explore, move, manipulate, smell, touch and repeat as they learn."

15. Establish a "No TV after 8:00" or similar rule.

16. Rather than have children rush through homework or chores to watch a particular program, record it so it can be watched at a better time.

17. Watch TV with your children and discuss the program content, including the implications of the commercials.

This stuff isn't easy, but much of parenting isn't. Keep your eyes on the goal. Let your kids be kids. Be patient. Don't give up. Help make your house the happiest place on the block to come home to.

I love this song; I want my kids to be able to sing it to me. It was made popular in the U.S. by Josh Groban. Here are the words of the chorus, I encourage you to go to the website I've listed below and listen to him sing it with backup by the African Children's Choir. It's a meltdown moment.

> You raise me up so I can stand on mountains;
> You raise me up to walk on stormy seas;
> I am strong when I am on your shoulders;
> You raise me up to more than I can be.[14]

As a Dad, that's my role. That's my privilege. That's my challenge. I love it.

14 http://www.youtube.com/watch?v=0OOhd6R2EiY

CHAPTER 6

A HOUSEFUL OF LAUGHTER

Laughter makes some people really nervous.

If there's laughter in the classroom, they reason, can there be much learning going on? If there's laughter in the workplace, can folks really be tending to business? If there's laughter in the home, can the kids really be getting the training they need? If there's laughter in the church, is there genuine spirituality there? (Maybe the folks just don't understand the seriousness of the situation.)

We ought to drive our kids bonkers with the joy they see in us.

See, I think we ought to drive our kids bonkers with the joy they see in us. Joy is not only contagious—it's attractive.

One of the most convincing evidences that you're on to something big is when there is frequent, hardy laughter in your house. Parents learning to laugh at themselves. Turning assignments into games. Laughing your way through spilled milk and misplaced keys.

We've been through some pretty heavy stuff in the preceding pages, and it's not uncommon to read a parenting book and see it as a grueling journey. You finish reading and you go, *Whew!* Fact is, like any worthwhile journey, there are sunny days and some cloudy ones.

Question: What memories will the young people who leave your home and establish their own have of their growing-up years?

Quite often when I'm chatting with parents my first suggestion will be, "Lighten up." Some moms and dads live in mortal dread that they are going to commit some single horrendous parenting gaffe and scar their kids for life. So they ratchet up the intensity, apply every rule they can remember, and go through the day as focused as a lifeguard at a busy pool.

I remember reading the story of a little boy—maybe 3 or 4—who was getting the milk out of the refrigerator when he dropped the carton. It hit the floor, splashed all over the place, and lay on its side *goodle-goodling* a puddle of milk beside the kitchen table.

What's a mom to do? What would you do?

Here's what this mom did. She picked up the carton and then said something like, "Well, that's one of the biggest messes I've seen for a long time. I think we ought to enjoy that mess before we clean it up, don't you? Take off your shoes and see how it feels to walk around in milk when you're barefooted. Then we'll clean it up." Lighten up. There's a world of difference between a little accident and a fist-shaking rebellion. We can leave our kids with few more valuable legacies than a childhood filled with happy memories.

I didn't know my dad could dance like that.

We were having dinner at my parents' place one summer when our sons were probably 11 and 8. As someone passed a large dish of green beans to my dad, he didn't have a good hold of it and it slipped out of his hands, hit the edge of the table, and landed upside down . . . in his lap. The beans were hot. I didn't know he could dance like that.

Mom got towels and started mopping up the juice; someone came with a dustpan and began scooping up the beans. Dad dribbled bean juice down the hall to change clothes.

When everyone returned to the table to resume the meal, it was our 8-year-old who broke the silence. "I'm glad it wasn't me that dropped the beans," he observed, "or I would sure have got in trouble." Unfortunately, he was probably right. But that event helped me to remember to distinguish between an accident and a rebellious spirit in dealing with my kids. Accidents are part of being human; that reality needs to temper my response.

Is it always going to be deliriously happy around your house? As the kids say, "Get real!" Actually, I prefer the word "joyous" to "happy" anyway. Happy is related to "happen" or "chance," and it most accurately describes the attitude of one who is affected by what "happens" around them. True joy, on the other hand, is not affected by circumstances. Not by wealth or poverty, not by sickness or health.

Our kids are helped as much by watching their parents' stable, joyous attitude as they are by about anything we do. Remember, joy is contagious.

Joy exists best where people like each other. I know, I know, *love* is a bigger word. But you can love someone and not like them.

A few days ago I was following a little group—two kids, maybe 5 and 7, and two adults, probably Mom and Grandma—through a supermarket. It was painful. Mom never stopped talking long enough to breathe, and Grandma's face was colonized by a huge scowl that by this point in her life was permanently encamped there. I felt so sorry for the kids I could have cried. They didn't have a chance.

The kids were energetic but not unruly, full of life but not boisterous. "Stop that. Don't. Come over here. Put that down. No, you can't. Let go of him. Shut up. I've told you a thousand times. Wait'll I get you home. You're gonna get it. We're not gonna stop and get ice cream." And those are just the ones I remember.

Judging by the aura around their shopping cart, I doubt that things got much better when they got out to the car, or when they got home. I don't know how long it had been since the four of them had had a good laugh together, but judging by the atmosphere they created going down the aisle, my hunch is that it had been a while. They deserve better, both the kids and the adults.

When I was in graduate school I read a book—a huge book, maybe 500 or 600 pages—entitled simply *Laughter*. It wasn't funny, but then it wasn't intended to be. It was an analysis of the reasons people laugh. I had never stopped to analyze it before; why do people laugh?

Like a lot of the books I read in grad school, I don't remember much about it. Except this: The thesis of the book was that laughter is really a negative event because it is usually a form of derision directed at others. Is that true? Well, there are mother-in-law jokes and blond jokes and Polish jokes. So I guess some humor is at others' expense.

But not all. Wasn't it Rodney Dangerfield who made a fortune making people laugh at his self put-downs? And some laughter is not about people at all . . . There are jokes about the weather, about old cars, about money, about any topic you could mention.

So here's why I took a whole chapter to talk about laughter in a book on parenting: People are helped to bond when they share a meal, share tears, and share laughter. One summer about 1970 my two sons and I (I think they were 15 and 12) drove a Volkswagen from the state of Washington cross-country to Ohio. If anyone asks, you can tell them that's a long trip in a non-air-conditioned Volkswagen. Actually, in July that's a long trip in a non-air-conditioned *anything*.

The assignment was that we were each to come up with an idea for a new invention that no one would ever need.

Somewhere about midway, I think it was central South Dakota (man, it's a long way across South Dakota), we invented a new game to help pass the time. The assignment was that we were each to come up with an idea for a new invention that no one would ever need. Some of them were hilarious. I still remember two of them—a trailer hitch for an airplane and screen doors for a submarine. We laughed so hard I thought we were going to have to pull over and stop.

Not long ago the three of us were reminiscing about that trip. We remembered the game and began recalling some of those bizarre inventions, and even though it was more than 40 years later—and this time we were sitting safely on the front porch—we laughed till we could hardly breathe. That four-day trip remains, for all three of us, one of the great adventures of their growing-up years.

And have you noticed how you can often defuse a volatile situation with a little humor? When our younger son, Randy, was 6, he woke up one morning feeling really punk. Closer examination revealed that he had an elevated temp and was covered with red spots. Chicken pox.

He was one unhappy dude. He felt awful, had to miss school, and had to stay in bed. We listened to him fuss for a little bit while we tried to convince him that it truly was chicken pox and that he would be out of commission for several days. That only ratcheted up the anguish he was feeling.

I would pay a hundred dollars cash if I had a picture of the look on his face when he saw the egg.

I slipped out of his room and went to the refrigerator. I got an egg and placed it carefully in my pocket. I returned to his bed and pretended to be straightening his covers; then while he was distracted I slipped the egg in his bed. After a moment I said, "You know, one way we can be sure it truly is chicken pox is if there is . . ." and I pulled the covers back. I would pay a hundred dollars cash if I had a picture of the look on his face when he saw the egg. "Yup," I said, "it's chicken pox all right."

We still laugh about it.

That wasn't the end of the saga. In a couple of days he was still pretty sick and he developed a deep, hacking cough that worried us. The doctor told us we needed to make sure he stayed in bed until his fever subsided and the spots began to fade. But remember, the boy was 6.

As a parent, you know that a high-energy 6-year-old and staying in bed when the sun is shining are two totally incompatible entities. We would make the orders very clear and walk out of his room. Almost before the echo of our footsteps died out he would be up playing with his toys or in some other fashion attempting to subvert our get-well instructions. And coughing. That was our biggest concern. The last thing we wanted to have happen was for this thing to morph into pneumonia.

So I thought to myself, *Self, let's be creative here . . .*

I walked into his room, scooted him back into his bed again, and sat on the edge of it. I said something like, "Look, if we don't get this thing under control, you're going to end up coughing your head off, and I was wondering if you had any idea of some of the complications that is going to cause.

"For instance, when we go to Disneyland, if your head is missing, you will be too short to ride on some of your favorite rides. You won't be able to eat because you won't have a mouth . . . and you know how you like Mom's cooking. When you get married [he was 6], you won't be able to kiss your wife because you won't have a face."

Then *he* started to get into it. "I won't be able to blow my nose," he contributed. "When I ride my bike down the street, I'll run into stuff because I can't see where I'm going."

"You may not be able to get a driver's license," I added. I don't remember how long this foolishness went on, but we were both in stitches.

Long story short, he got the point. The won't-stay-in-bed crisis was behind us. That night at supper Jerry, his older brother, asked what all the racket was coming out of Randy's room. I told the story of our laugh-in, and then Jerry started to pick it up. "At least he won't have to go to the dentist," he noted. Randy would later say he thought it was the best sick he ever had.

"A cheerful heart is good medicine" (Proverbs 17:22). King Solomon wrote that nearly 3,000 years ago; I think he was on to something. There is much research now to demonstrate that laughter is good for our physical and emotional health. It's also good for the well-being of those in our families.

Joy is an attitude, and we choose our attitudes.

Here's an interesting question for you: Does a well-functioning family produce joy, or does joy produce a well-functioning family? Which is the chicken and which is the egg? Think about that, and we'll come back to it in a minute.

Joy is a decision. Joy is an attitude, and we choose our attitudes. Try smiling whenever you talk. Try smiling when you're on the phone. It changes the timbre of your voice. It changes how people feel about what you say. My wife often tells audiences, "When you smile, people think you're smarter than you are."

I have seldom received a compliment I cherish as much as the time recently when a young man named Jim approached Ruthie and me at church and said, "I've been watching you folks, and I think you must be the happiest people in our congregation." I don't know that it's true, but I'm glad Jim saw something that made him think so. I really believe that because joy is a decision, it is one of the prime ingredients in building a well-functioning family. Whether that's the chicken or the egg, I'll leave that decision up to you.

But it works the other way, too. A well-functioning family is a joyous place to be. Think about the four people I described earlier in the aisle of the supermarket. A perpetually sour countenance does not create a joyous place to grow up.

Do you remember the happy banter of the Mary Poppins movie? I love one of the songs she sings called "A Spoonful of Sugar." If you have seen the movie, you'll remember the lyrics in which she talks about, of all things, common household chores. She reminds us that "in every job that must be done there is an element of fun." And she says that tasks we undertake can become "a piece of cake." Then she sings that famous line: "a spoonful of sugar helps the medicine go down."

Lest you think I'm trivializing the family nutrition schedule, rest assured that I'm not. Leaders create the atmosphere in the organization they manage. As a leader, you do that too. So be honest now—what's the atmosphere in your house? If you were to ask your kids to respond to that question by secret ballot, what would they say?

I know. They'd say something like, "I grew up in a houseful of laughter!" Well done!

CHAPTER 7

KUDZU PARENTS

Some people know it as "the vine that ate the South," and if you have driven around the southeastern United States much, you probably understand why. Most people know it as kudzu.

Kudzu was introduced into this country from Japan for our hundredth anniversary Centennial Celebration in Philadelphia in 1876. Since then it has developed a mixed reputation. Livestock will eat it, it can help manage soil erosion, its lush verdure is beautiful along roadsides during the growing season in the South, and several of its unique components are even used as ingredients in some exotic medicines.

But it can grow 60 feet in a single growing season—up to a foot a day—it's extremely difficult to eradicate, and it kills virtually every living thing that serves as its host. It is estimated to currently cover more than 7,000,000 acres of the southeastern United States.

Ruthie and I have been intrigued as we have traveled throughout the South to see the power poles, barns, unused chicken sheds, and even vehicles that have been totally engulfed by its rich vegetation. Not long ago we passed a small empty house near the road in north Georgia that was totally covered with kudzu. Ruthie said, "Apparently those folks don't get out much." We stopped and took a photo.

The biggest downside of kudzu is the extent to which it ravages any living thing it climbs on. It's almost like a parasite as it shuts out the sunlight and steals the nutrients. So when a kudzu vine dies back in the late fall, the trees that were its host have had the life sucked out of them.

I recite all of this horticultural trivia to make this point: *I talk to a lot of kudzu parents.* On the surface all is well. Beautiful, in fact. Serene. But underneath is a Smother Mother (and/or Dad), sucking the life out of Junior. These are the parents who raise their kids as resident celebrities, asking nothing of them, eager to wait on them hand and foot, requiring nothing of them, and unwilling to hand over increasingly significant chores. They manage every minute of every day for their child. They attempt to determine who their child's friends will be. They tell them when to get up and when to eat breakfast; they chase them around the house to get them out the door to the school bus on time.

Micromanagement does to people what kudzu does to trees.

"Go over your spelling words again, or you might not pass the test tomorrow." "Time to practice your piano, or Mrs. Evans will really be upset." "Put on your coat; it's cold outside." "Put your bike away, honey; I think it's going to rain." It's called micromanagement, and it does to people what kudzu does to trees.

The tainted logic behind this kind of high-presence supervisory parenting is the assumption that if Mom and Dad write the script, call the shots, pull the strings, and hover over the field of play, Johnny is going to be happy and the family will live stress-free.

Even if it were true, that's a short-term perspective.

Here's what Alicia, a wise mother of four—a non-kudzu mother—wrote to me recently.

> I am looking for places in my kids' lives to support them in age-appropriate decisions—and let them benefit from the consequences, whether positive or negative. Like when they were going away to camp last summer . . .

We made a list of what they would need and I told
them I was available as they got their stuff together. But I
determined that I was *not* going to check their bags before
they left. That was really hard but I knew they would learn
more if they got there without things they needed than
they would learn if I double-checked everything.

Smart mom. And Alicia's right; that's really hard for most of
us. We want to be "good" parents. We want to spare our kids any
unnecessary discomfort. We want to smooth the way for them and
let them learn from the mistakes of others rather than their own. The
truth is, attitudes and habits learned young are generally the ones that
shape our actions, often for life.

I've been interested to watch parents who struggle and connive to
get their kids into a "Gifted and Talented" program at school; then
when the kids come home they treat them as though they're hard of
hearing or can't follow simple instructions.

Why would any youngster need to be told more than once to do a chore?

Why would any youngster need to be told more than once to do
a chore?

"Well, because he doesn't do it the first time I tell him."

"Really? Why?"

"I don't know—it's a habit, I guess."

Want to get him over the habit? It's not that hard.

For instance, Freddie is 12, and mornings are a consistent
nightmare. You begin trying to wake him at 6:15. At 6:30 you check,
and he's still in bed; he covers his head with the pillow when you come
into his room. You raise your voice enough to be heard and alert him to
the fact that if he doesn't roll out "right now," he's going to be late.

Freddie begrudgingly agrees and stirs beneath the covers, enough at least to let you know he's alive. You tell him that breakfast is on the table and he needs to hurry. "OK, Mom," you hear him say from under the pillow.

It's 6:40, and there haven't been many noises from Freddie's room, so you venture in again. Same unmoving blob under the covers. This time you ramp up the urgency and add a few threats to make sure he gets it. By now it's 10 minutes to 7:00, and . . . well, you could perhaps write the rest of that script. Or play it back from this morning's scenario?

Let's visualize a new version: After dinner Dad and Mom tell Freddie they have an announcement. Accompanied by a little bit of drama, they tell him that they have a gift for him that is going to change his life. They hand him a small gift-wrapped box. Eagerly and with some excitement Freddie tears off the wrapping paper and discovers—an alarm clock.

"What's this about?" asks Freddie.

"Well," Dad replies, "we have decided we have not been treating you as a 12-year-old should be treated. We have been hounding you and making your mornings miserable. But that's over. The bus comes at 7:30, so you need to be out the front door by 7:25.

"Before that, you'll need to get ready, do morning chores, eat breakfast, brush your teeth, grab your books, and be on your way. So set the alarm for whatever amount of time you need, and you're on your own."

"But Dad, what if I sleep through the alarm?"

"Well, you can ride your bike to school in less than 40 minutes, or if you're really running late or it's raining, you could call a cab."

"Yeah, right. Do you know how much a cab costs?"

"I'm not sure; probably not more than $10 or $15."

"How would I pay for *that*?"

"Well, you might need to salt a little away out of your allowance just in case."

"Dad, do you know what the penalty is for an unexcused absence at school?"

"Well, you won't need to *miss* the class; you'd just be *tardy*."

"But it's the same penalty as if I'm absent—it lowers my grade."

"Whoa, do you think that could have some long-term effect on your getting into the seventh grade next year?"

"Dad, this just isn't fair."

"Not fair? What's not fair about it?"

"You know I need help getting up in the morning."

"That's why we bought you the alarm clock. Be sure you set it after you plug it in. Like we said, it'll change your life."

A note of caution here: After a major adjustment like this one, things can sometimes get worse before they start getting better. Sometimes much worse. Be strong.

Then is it worth it? Well, here is a better question: Which is more important—that Freddie get to his first-period class on time because his mom hounded him, or that he learns to be a self-starter? That he not have any unexcused absences in the sixth grade, or that he goes into the seventh grade able to take responsibility for his own actions?

A woman who had attended a John Rosemond coaching seminar wrote to us, telling us that in the seminar she learned that her 9-year-old needed to develop some responsibility of his own. Here is what she said:

I came home (from the seminar) and out of habit, immediately began micro-managing my 9-year-old to get ready for school in the morning. But I stopped dead in my tracks, apologized to him for treating him like a dummy and told him he knows exactly what he needs to do to get ready. I told him the cut off for being ready was 7:10 am.

So far, he has been ready every morning with one exception... and that was when he learned that 7:11 was too late.

I have not screamed, yelled, nagged or berated him since I got back from the seminar. I have finally internalized that his problems are NOT my problems.

I have now added daily chores to his to-do list... This morning, he did not feed the dog as asked, I simply went ahead, did it myself and then told him later that there would be a consequence for not doing his chores. When he complains, which he sometimes still does, I have not taken the bait. I just shrug my shoulders and move on. It has totally changed the atmosphere in our home.

Often in these pages I have trumpeted how essential it is to build respect into the relationship between parents and kids and between kids and parents. Mom and Dad set the tone on this project.

You might want to copy this paragraph and tape it to the bathroom mirror.

Follow this closely, please . . . huge issue coming up: *Micromanaging is a sign of lack of trust.* By our actions we can imply, "I don't *trust* you to remember to feed the dog," "I don't *trust* you to get ready on time," "I don't *trust* you to wear your coat," "I don't *trust* you to get your homework done." *And lack of trust is one of the loudest evidences of lack of respect.* Let me turn it around: When we show them that we trust them, it builds their self-respect, and it helps them learn to respect us. (You might want to copy that paragraph and tape it to the bathroom mirror.)

But isn't it true that trust is earned? Yes, it is. But this is also true: Kids tend to live up to the reputation we give them. So the more trust toward them we can demonstrate, the sooner they will learn to act in ways that earn that trust.

And remember, it is during this 3-to-teen window that we need to build those traits that produce a teen who (1) can manage him/herself, (2) understands the everything-I-do-has-a-consequence reality, and (3) has figured out that his/her greatest satisfaction comes from being a contributing member of society. Those traits don't appear by accident; they grow from seeds that Mom and Dad intentionally nurture.

And mutual respect is a by-product. That's a really big deal.

BEAR TRAPS AND BARE FEET

As a parent, what can I do to guarantee that my kids make the right choices?

Fact is, of course, there are no guarantees in the kid business. And you and I didn't make all the right choices when we were growing up either. How many times did your dad shake his head or your mom throw up her hands in dismay?

Yeah, mine too.

So forget this "all the right choices" business. Our goal here is to focus on getting as near as we can to a desired outcome, knowing there will be hiccups en route. We can prewrite the goals, but we can't prewrite the script. And when you find yourself struggling with guilt because your kids made a bad decision, I encourage you to recall the Bible story of Adam and Eve. According to the account, although Adam had the ideal father—God—he still made some bad choices.

OK, that helps.

The title of this book—*Rare Kids; Well Done*—was not chosen because it had catchy words in it or because of its double entendre, but because it said what we wanted to say: We all have *rare kids* (right?), and when they hit full stride, we want to be able to look back at the contribution we've made and feel like the job we did was, well, *well done.*

You can say that because you don't know my kids.

"Yeah, Dr. Don . . . you can say that because *your* kids are grown, and besides, you don't know *my* kids."

No, I don't know your kids, but here's what I *do* know. Because you are reading this book, I know that you are committed to coaching your kids through the minefields—including those that are unique to the twenty-first century—so they come out the other side as joyous, healthy, effective change agents with as few regrets as possible. That's a great perspective from which to view tomorrow.

Have you seen the Promise Keepers' exercise that illustrates that vision? It's awesome. On this huge stage, surrounded by a stadium full of maybe 50,000 or more dads, one of the speakers places a bunch of steel bear traps, already set, around on the floor of the stage. The traps are close enough together that you'd have to be really careful just to walk between them.

Then a teen is brought onto the stage—we'll call him Jason. Just the idea of how much damage one of those traps could do to a foot and ankle if the boy were to try to walk across the stage and then got careless creates palpable tension in the stadium.

The speaker's theme is to illustrate the reality of the traps and the dangers that stalk every teen's journey. "Jason," the speaker begins, "to make my point, I'd like for you to walk across the stage through the traps. Barefoot!"

Jason unenthusiastically begins to remove his shoes...

After a minute Jason unenthusiastically begins to remove his shoes and looks at the gaping traps. He ponders a minute, swallows hard, then replies that he is willing, but only reluctantly. One misstep, one careless instant, and he might lose a toe . . .

Finally Jason prepares to take a first tentative step; the speaker asks him to wait. The crowd watches in disbelief as the speaker goes to Jason and ties a blindfold over his face, completely covering his eyes. Suddenly the dynamics on the stage change dramatically.

You can sense the crowd holding its collective breath. No one speaks. No one moves. No one blinks. Call it corporate focus.

Now what will Jason do? More hesitantly this time, he steadies himself to measure his treacherous walk through the steel traps. Several seconds pass. Just as he is contemplating taking a first tenuous step, he hears an urgent voice: "Jason, stop!" It's Jason's dad.

Quickly the dad walks around the edge of the stage and stands facing his blindfolded son. Putting the boy's hands on his own broad shoulders, Dad begins to guide him slowly, carefully, through the maze, coaching at every step. "OK, a little to the right . . . Now a slow arc left . . . Follow my lead . . . Careful here . . . You're doing great . . . Almost there . . ." Then, "Made it!"

Fifty thousand men exhale, wipe their tears, then erupt in a thunderous ovation.

I know you get it. That's our role, isn't it? That's why we may often find ourselves holding our breath and wiping our eyes in the real world, too.

Let's see if we can put a title on our role: Which term do you like best?

☐ Guide ☐ Coach ☐ Trailblazer
☐ Helper ☐ Mentor ☐ Escort

Whichever defines it best for you, there is the distinct sense in all of us that the stakes are much higher after we leave the stage for the real world. But we are *urged on* by our unshakeable love for our kids. And we are *made useful* by the fact that we have been through the traps before; thus we can see some things our kids can't see.

My mom and dad divorced when I was 6, and my mom and I were alone together for the next seven or eight years. But my mom often told me wonderful stories her dad had told her about his dad. Stories about hard work. About his loyalty to his family. About walking four miles in a heavy North Carolina rain to return 10 cents, which the clerk at the country store had accidentally overpaid him in change.

Every decision we make is not about what we will do; it's about who we are.

Your kids will tell their kids stories about you. And that generation will tell them to the next. Give them big stories to tell. Stories about character. Stories about values. Stories about the exhilaration of taking the high road. Stories of risks taken for the right reasons. Stories about wise choices you made and dumb choices you made, and how they can tell the difference. And why the difference matters.

Help them see the truth about consequences: Every decision they make has consequences. Every decision. No amount of wishing can change that. Every decision we make is not about what we will do; it's about who we are. And very often those consequences involve others. Ruthie and I were driving recently near Jacksonville, Florida, and saw a billboard that said: "Abortion: Ten minutes to have one; a lifetime to regret it." Not every choice has as far-reaching repercussions as that one, but the principle is still true: Every decision has consequences.

That helps me put a definition on one of our most rewarding assignments as dads and moms—and grandparents: *We are trap navigators for a barefoot generation.* Showing the way. Guiding the steps. Coaching the choices. Seeking to get these precious kids from one side of life's stage to the other still intact.

But more than helping them just survive the journey, we can help them dream great dreams. We can help them learn to be far-horizon thinkers. We can open up options for their future that they may never have thought of. We can steady them when the uncertainties of adolescence seem to overwhelm. We can help them grasp the mind-expanding reality that they have been put here for a purpose and that they will find the greatest satisfaction and fulfillment and joy as they discover that purpose and watch it come to full bloom before their eyes.

A high percentage of the young adults you meet can tell you how their parents either taught them all the reasons they needed to be cautious or sought to open up exciting possibilities to them, helping them to see, as Ginger the hen says in the movie *Chicken Run,* "The fences are all in your head!"

What I am hoping will happen in this chapter is that it will help reset the bar for us as parents. If we're going to be part of nurturing a mind-boggling vision in the hearts of our kids, we've got to be driven by a ginormous (pronounced jy-normus) vision of our own as to what we can bring to the process.

So let's do some "There is no limit . . ." thinking for a minute. A friend sent me this story from the Internet, so who knows whether it's true. If you don't think so, just call it a parable, but catch the vision of this young educator. The article is entitled "What Do Teachers Make?"

The dinner guests were sitting around the table discussing life. One man, the CEO of a large company, decided to explain the problem with education. He argued, "What's a kid going to learn from someone who decided his best option in life was to become a teacher?" He reminded the other dinner guests what they say about teachers: "Those who can, do. Those who can't, teach."

To stress his point he said to another guest, "You're a teacher, Bonnie. Be honest. What do you make?"

Bonnie, who had a reputation for honesty and frankness, replied, "You want to know what I make?" She paused for a second, then began...

"Well, I make kids work harder than they ever thought they could. I make a C+ feel like the Congressional Medal of Honor. I make kids sit through forty minutes of class time when their parents can't make them sit for five without an iPod, Game Cube, or movie rental.

"You want to know what I make," she continued, pausing again to look at everyone around the table. "I make kids wonder. I make them question. I make them apologize and mean it. I make them have respect and take responsibility for their actions. I teach them to write and then I make them write.

"Keyboarding isn't everything. I make them read, read, read. I make them show all their work in math. They use their God-given brain, not a man-made calculator.

"I make my students from other countries learn everything in English while preserving their unique cultural identity. I make my classroom a place where all my students feel safe.

"I make my students stand, placing their hand over their heart to say the Pledge of Allegiance to the flag, One Nation Under God, because we live in the United States of America.

"Finally, I make them understand that if they use the gifts they were given, work hard, and follow their hearts, they can succeed in life." She paused one last time and then continued.

"Then when people try to judge me by what I make, with me knowing money isn't everything, I can hold my head up high and pay no attention because they are ignorant.

"You want to know what I make? I MAKE A DIFFERENCE! What do you make, Mr. CEO?"

His jaw dropped; he went silent.

Have you met my friend Rafe Esquith? (No, I didn't get my fingers on the wrong row of keys; that *is* his name.) Rafe is a fifth-grade teacher in a large inner-city school (which he calls "the jungle") in Los Angeles. Most of his students are from low-income families of recent immigrants.[15]

The theme of his homeroom and all that goes on there is "No Shortcuts."

The vision Rafe is able to build into their hearts during their fifth year of school leaves you staring at the wall with your mouth open. What I want you to know right now about his mentoring of 11- and 12-year-olds is this: The theme of his homeroom and all that goes on

15 Rafe Esquith, Teach Like Your Hair Is On Fire, (New York, Pantheon Press) 2007

Bear Traps and Bare Feet

there is "No Shortcuts." As you and I embark on this parenting saga together, it needs to be our motto, too. No shortcuts. I hope you'll let it marinate in your heart for a bit.

I have industrial-strength respect for people who run marathons. Twenty-six-and-two-tenths miles of numb-making torment. It tests your focus, your heart, your lungs, your knees, your feet. Oh, and did I mention your focus? And it's not just the race; it's the months of solo agony building the stamina and dealing with the pain to even qualify to compete. You don't have to win to be a hero in my book; if you finish, you're a winner.

Rosie Ruiz, a Cuban, was the first woman competitor to cross the finish line of the 84th Boston Marathon in 1980. Her world-record-setting time of 2:31:56 immediately vaulted her into global prominence in the athletic world.

But there were some questions.

For instance, some of the spectators reported that they had not seen her running at the beginning of the race. Though she was registered to compete, she did not appear in videotape footage at the start. A spectator from the crowd, then others, came forward to corroborate that they had seen her run into the race near the 25-mile point. When asked by a reporter how she had run the grueling race and didn't seem to be fatigued, Rosie replied that she just "got up with a lot of energy" that morning.

An interesting sidebar on the story is that to qualify to run in the Boston, a runner must finish in appropriate time in the New York Marathon that precedes it. Rosie had presented herself at the first aid station at the finish of the New York race and reported that she had finished but had injured herself. Volunteers marked her down as having completed the marathon and thereby qualified for the Boston.

But Rosie Ruiz was stripped of her Boston Marathon title, and it was given to a Canadian who had finished just behind her. I don't recall ever hearing of Rosie Ruiz since.

Rafe Esquith reminds us that there are no shortcuts. Too bad Rosie could not have been in his fifth-grade class. I've wondered who was her coach? I've wondered if her dad or mom were out there with her on her practice runs. Who was there to bring out the best in her? Who was there cheering her on, reminding her that in all competition it is not winning that counts in the final analysis—it's the magnificence of the struggle.

Just as it is appropriate to say that there are no guarantees in the kid business, it is also correct to say that *there are no shortcuts*. Maybe that's our first channel marker.

CHAPTER 9

SOMEWHERE NORTH OF RESPECT

Until I was thirteen, I thought my name was "shut up!"

-Joe Namath

Earlier in the book I made some pretty strident claims as to the value of *respect*. We're going to get into it again here, and I promise you'll see it again before we're finished. I feel very keenly about this, and I hope you do too.

When Alvin was 11 he was a bit overweight . . . No, he was fat. Not huge fat, just fat. Whenever his mom bought clothes for him (we need to talk about that), she always bought him T-shirts. And they were always *tight*.

Now, tight T-shirts were not flattering to Alvin. Not only did they show every roll, but also they emphasized places where no boy likes to have places. His buddies made fun; the girls snickered.

Alvin began compensating by wearing a coat even when it was warm; even when it was hot. True, it looked strange, but it was better than the embarrassment of revealing contours he desperately wished he didn't have.

More than once Alvin started to talk about the T-shirt thing with his folks. But they were not willing to be a part of the conversation. Their words were something like "You unappreciative brat; you ought to be thankful we buy you new clothes at all." True story.

Time for a definition . . .

Respect: *the act of treating another person with dignity and fairness.* Granted, that's *my* definition, but it's a good one.

I still open the car door for her whenever we are going somewhere together.

Ruthie and I have been married for a long time—a bunch of decades now—and I still open the car door for her whenever we are going somewhere together. Sometimes I have the feeling that people watch us and say to themselves, "Look at that older couple and the way they're acting; they must be newlyweds."

Maybe it's a generational thing—my era was more apt to do that kind of thing than this one—but I think it's more than that. To me it's a matter of respect. I value her. I am honored to have her as part of my life. She's one of the two or three most important things that have ever happened to me. I want to make sure she knows it, and the car door thing is just one of scads of ways I've discovered by which I can remind her.

Once when our older son was a toddler he was acting up in church. In a huff I grabbed him gruffly by the arm and took him outside. I doubt that he remembers the incident; he may not even know about it till he reads it here. But I was ashamed afterward, and I vowed I would never again show that kind of disrespect to my kids.

By the way, he's a dad now—may even be a granddad by the time this book goes to press—and I learned a lot from him by watching him dad his two daughters. You've heard the impatient mom or dad at the supermarket bark at their youngster (why is it so often in their outdoor voice?): "You put that down and get over here right now!" What I usually heard our son say to his girls was something like "Come here, please, and let's put the jar of pickles back where it was." Dignity. Respect. I love it.

On a billboard near Hayesville, North Carolina, not far from our home, is a picture of a cherubic little girl in a car seat. The caption says, "Every time you yell at another driver, she learns something." Respect is both caught and taught. So reflect with me how consistently you and I treat everyone in our world with respect . . . dignity and fairness.

Leon, in seventh grade, doesn't get his homework done. *Consistently* he doesn't get his homework done. His grades aren't good; the teacher keeps sending notes home, and his mother and dad hound him almost every evening. But there is no observable change.

Question: Is what you're doing working? Not well? Then are you open to exploring other options? Let me suggest one . . .

Leon comes home with a note saying that he didn't get his history paper finished. Again. Leon is primed for the lecture. It's a nightly ritual; he could write the script: "Go to your room and finish that history lesson, and don't come out till it's *done!* Oh, and no TV!"

Rest assured that we're not going to be hounding you about it anymore.

What if, since that script hasn't worked very well, Mom or Dad would say simply, unemotionally, "Leon, have you thought about having to take that history class over next year? Or maybe summer school instead of going to camp? You need it to get into the eighth grade, you know. You probably aren't going to want to do that, so, well, you'll know what to do about it. You're really the only one who can solve the problem, and we believe you will. And rest assured that we're not going to be hounding you about it anymore."

That simple strategy illustrates a *powerful principle* that can produce a dramatic change in your child's behavior as well as in the atmosphere in your home.

See, two really important things happen downwind of that exchange. Leon has it reinforced that he is the one in charge of the choices in his life, that he creates his own outcomes. And second, Mom and Dad have been able to confront the homework issue and still leave his dignity intact. They've surfaced the issue, but they have not compromised the respect they always want to give him. They're not stressed; he better understands the outcome of the choices he has to make. Seems like everybody wins.

You may be thinking, *But what if it doesn't work?* (And remember that often, following this kind of precipitous midcourse correction, things get worse before they begin to get better.) OK, so what's the worst thing that could happen? He'd be embarrassed. You'd be embarrassed. He might even be held back a year in school.

Question: How important is it to you that Leon discovers the relationship between his choices and the consequences? How important is it to you—and to Leon—that he becomes self-motivated, that the outcomes of his decisions become a product of *his* plan for his life and not *your* plan for his life? How much discomfort are you willing to tolerate in order for him to learn one of the most important lessons he'll ever learn? In your game plan, which is the more important for Leon—that he gets a good grade in history class or that he learns responsibility?

It's common for parents to badger their kids in the hopes that the kids' conduct won't cause undesired outcomes and/or embarrass Mom or Dad. (I mean, what will Grandma say when she learns that Leon "flunked history"?) Problem is, that route very often degenerates into a full-blown battle in which the child's resentment is directed at Mom and Dad—who don't really own the problem.

Let's put another vignette in the projector . . . a "What if . . .?" What if, after a couple of reminders to bring her bike in, 9-year-old Cindy leaves it out in the front yard—again—and it rains . . . hard. Since the bike is her responsibility, Mom and Dad don't rescue her by bringing it in to the garage for her.

No bike is as important as the relationship dad and mom
want to maintain with Cindy

A few days later she wants to take a bike ride with a couple of friends. She remembers her bike. It's still outside. Wet. The hand brakes won't work, and the seat is soaked.

You know the drill . . . "Daaddd, my bike won't work. Will you fix it?"

Dad takes a look and says, "Honey, I'm sorry, but the cables that work the front and back brakes are rusted, and you can't ride a bike with no brakes."

"Daaddd, what should I do? Will you buy some new ones?"

"Well, Cindy, I'm really sorry, but they're only ruined because the bike was left out in the rain. Since that was your decision, it means it will be up to you to solve the problem. If you want to buy some new ones, I'll help you put them on, though."

"But then I can't go riding with my friends today."

"I know, honey; that's a bummer, isn't it? But you're creative, so you can probably think of something else fun to do with your friends."

See all the healthy stuff that's going on here?

- Cindy is learning responsibility.

- She is discovering that her choices have consequences—and there was no lecture.

- Mom and Dad haven't used up their coaching collateral by nagging her to bring in her bike. The bike didn't become the focus of a shouting match.

- They have treated her with respect—dignity and fairness.

- If Cindy is upset with anyone, it is likely herself, not her parents.

- Mom and Dad are feeling gratified that they didn't allow the bicycle incident to escalate into World War III. No bike is as important as the relationship Dad and Mom want to maintain with Cindy.

This bicycle thing is turning out to be a multi-facetted educational event

---

Oh, and wise parents that they are, they'll also make sure that Cindy pays for the bike parts herself from her allowance. "But, Dad, this week's allowance is all gone." Will Dad and Mom give her an advance? Nope. See, you never really learn how to manage money until you learn how to be broke. There's a little mechanism called Saving for a Rainy Day, and Cindy is just discovering how it works.

Or she may choose to rake leaves or sell lemonade or develop some other entrepreneurial skills. You know, this bicycle thing is turning out to be a multifaceted educational event; all the while Cindy is discovering that her parents believe in her, trust her, love her. And that is the atmosphere in which a youngster comes to understand how people treat each other when they have deep respect for one another.

Here's the deal: One of the most important things that must happen between parents and their kids—one of the issues Dad and Mom must really invest themselves in—is keeping the communication intact. *No issue is so vast that it is worth sacrificing the parent-child relationship.*

The kids who open up with parents and discuss the really heavy stuff they're processing are not the kids who get hammered when they make a mistake. Keep the dialogue open when they're 9, and it'll likely still be open when they're 16.

Robby knows that Mom and Dad are going to be disappointed when they learn that he stole a calculator from a classmate's backpack. But he knows he will not be berated or trounced. Rather, he knows that restitution, apology, and the proper discipline will be processed and that when the incident is over, he and his parents will still be friends.

A 30-something friend whom I deeply admire recently wrote to me reflecting on his teen years:

> For me, the biggest reason I didn't do drugs, etc., was because I didn't want to let my parents down. Not friends, not what people would think of me, but my parents.

When we learn to watch for them, these kinds of teachable moments are everywhere. They don't require a scolding, a shouting match, a threat, or an argument. Just a *Rare Kids; Well Done* attitude and a wise parent or two.

But this chapter is entitled "Somewhere North of Respect."

Where is that? Thanks for reminding me. *Respect* is such a nonnegotiable in a family—in all of our relationships, really—that I wanted to make sure we nailed it down pretty tight before we left.

When you respect someone, you don't yell at them

When you respect someone, you don't yell at them. I mean, you and I both know that it's not easy to learn to respect someone who yells at you. When you respect someone, you don't swear at them. You don't call them names. You don't compare them to others. You don't embarrass them in front of their friends. You don't traffic in put-downs.

But north of respect, beyond respect, the other side of respect, what does it look like there? Big term coming up. Huge term:

HONOR

I told you it was a big word. If you're in a running tiff right now with your teen or tween, the idea of *respect* may have caused you to feel close to the brink. The idea of conferring *honor* on that obstreperous alien who has set up camp in an upstairs bedroom may make it seem like it's about time to jump.

OK, let's see if we can work through that. First, let's come up with a working definition.

Honor. Well, it *doesn't* mean that you never make your children unhappy, never cross them, never discipline them, that you wait on them hand and foot, or that you rush to fill their every request. That's not honor; that's nonsense.

Honor does not mean allowing them to butt in to a conversation you're having with someone else, including when you're on the phone. It doesn't mean giving them their own menu for dinner, different from what the rest of the family is eating.

Once again, because honor is an attitude thing and we choose our attitudes, let's see if we can put some substance to the definition by doing a little "What if . . .?"

What if every teen knew that Mom and Dad would always treat them, not just with dignity and fairness, but with honor? *What if* every teen knew that their input would always be sought and valued in family decisions? *What if* every teen was made to feel that they were a special gift from God to their family? If that happened, would they feel respect? Maybe even honor?

Hey, wait, I like what you just said. I've never thought of it just like that.

What if, in the heat of an intense family discussion, you stopped and said something like "Hey, wait, I like what you just said. I've never thought of it just like that. I want to write that down before I forget it." Would that express respect, maybe even honor?

You affirm them, you show that you trust them, you assume the best about them, you give them all the decision-making room they are mature enough to handle. You create situations where they can make choices even beyond what they feel capable of. If that happened, would they feel respect? Maybe even honor?

Let's do a "for instance": Saturday night there's a basketball game at school. Leon (15) and some of his friends have worked out a plan. Orin (16) is going to pick them up about 7:00 in his folks' car; then off to the game.

So, Mom, Dad, let's think curfew here.

You show your love for Leon by asking where he's going to be, who he'll be with, and about when he plans to be home. Rather than your setting a time, what if you were to ask, "What time do you expect to be in?" "Well," Leon replies, "there's no school tomorrow, and we'd like to stop by the DQ, so how about an hour after the game?" "Deal," Dad says; "call us if your plans change." "Roger that," replies Leon.

Honor. An interesting word to use as you think about your teen. *Honor. It's kind of like respect on steroids.*

[CHAPTER 10]

DON'T FEAR WHEN A PEER APPEARS

In a 2010 survey by CASA (National Center on Addiction and Substance Abuse at Columbia University) 32 percent of American parents ranked *social pressure* as the biggest problem facing teens in school.[16]

I find that an amazing statistic. As nearly one out of three parents sees it, the "biggest problem" facing their kids in school is not drugs. It's not alcohol. It's not their teens being sexually active. It's not violence or schoolyard bullies. It's not texting while they're driving. It's not excessive homework. From the perspective of the parents who talk to their kids every day, who are worried about the influences their kids face as they deal with the behaviors that trouble them, their biggest concern is that influence that is responsible for many of those behaviors—peer pressure.

Ruthie and I were shopping in a Sam's Club in Columbia, South Carolina, recently and saw a little girl, maybe 4 years old, who was as cute as any I've seen in a long time (except for my two granddaughters, of course). I stepped up to the mother and told her I was impressed with her little one's behavior in a place where lots of kids are inclined to get pretty rowdy—shopping. She politely acknowledged her acceptance of my compliment.

I turned to walk away and heard a major commotion behind me. The little girl had apparently said something, and Mom had told her to be quiet. Mom grabbed her by the arm and shrieked out something like, "I HAVE TOLD YOU ALL I AM GOING TO TELL YOU THAT WHEN WE ARE IN HERE YOU ARE TO BE *QUIET!*" She shook her by the arm, and everyone in that end of the store cringed at the physical and verbal abuse of this little child.

Hopefully that mother will get help, and soon.

Hopefully that mother will get help, and soon. If she doesn't, before long her daughter will be old enough to seek out friends—peers—who

16 The "National Survey of American Attitudes on Substance Abuse XV: Teens and Parents" (PDF, 654 KB) is available online.

won't humiliate her in front of others. The daughter's attachment will move from the adult in her life who should be her source of respect and security to find comfort with some kids who will.

We've all had that moment when we wished we were somewhere else and didn't have to witness the mortification of a little kid. Or a big one. Some bleak day that mom will probably go to a pastor or counselor and say, "I just don't understand it . . . My teenage daughter won't listen to me anymore; she is disrespectful, and she won't do a thing I tell her. She spends all of her time with her friends, or on her cell phone with them or texting them . . . She won't even come to the table with us for supper. She grunts an answer when I ask her something. She doesn't want to go anywhere with the family—not even to church. Can you help me figure out what's wrong with her?"

We're sorry but not surprised, right?

Granted, the case I described may have been an extreme one, but the dynamics of the relationship the mother displayed are not that uncommon. But please write this big: There is no issue between parents and kids that is big enough to allow it to destroy the relationship between them.

When I opened the front door, a tall uniformed police officer stood there looking very displeased.

I know how it hurts. I think it was when I was 11 that I loaned a neighbor kid—Maynard—my BB gun. He was horsing around in the alley behind our house in Spokane, Washington, and shot another friend—Steven—in the face with it. The BB penetrated the skin of Steven's lower eyelid and sent him running down the street, holding his eye and bawling at the top of his lungs. I went in the house and sat down to think about what had just happened and wonder about my fate—and about Steven's eye.

Before long a car stopped out front, and there was a serious knock on the door. When I opened it, a tall uniformed police officer stood there looking very displeased. He asked me my name, asked me whether I had a BB gun, and then told me to come with him. He put me in the backseat of the car and drove away—to where, I didn't know. For how long, I didn't know.

A short time later we drove up in front of the Juvenile Detention Center on West Broadway, and the officer took me inside. A very stern woman asked me a lot of questions, then told me to take off my shoes. She took me upstairs, then down a long hallway, and opened the door to a small cell with two cots. Sitting on one of the cots was Maynard.

We spent a miserable night. The next morning, after breakfast, another woman with a perpetual scowl etched on her face came to the door and told me to come with her.

In the lobby at the foot of the steps my mother was waiting. I was so sorry for what had happened and so glad to see her that I rushed toward her with my arms outstretched. She turned her back and walked away.

No child should ever have to live with that memory.

We would reconcile later when she realized that my only "crime" had been loaning my BB gun to Maynard, who fired it inside the city limits, but her rejection haunted me for a long time. That's why I can say I know a little bit about how it hurts when kids sense that their folks have rejected them for something they have done. No child should ever have to live with that memory. I also began to understand a little more about why kids look for peers who will accept them when they feel that adults won't.

Let me see if I can put your mind at ease a bit here, though. First, parenting well will give you a far greater influence on the character and values of your kids than their peers will ever have. Second, peer influence is of surprisingly short duration. Little kids are less susceptible; older kids usually become more independent and begin making more of their own choices.

Usually, peer influence is felt most keenly during middle school. That's one of the reasons we've been talking so fervently about building values into our kids during that 3rd-to-13th birthday window. By the time our kids move past 12 into the teens, we need to make sure we have helped them move joyously and with a sense of satisfaction into a comfortable understanding of what our family deems valuable.

For the most part kids are drawn to those most like themselves.

And that segues into the third bit of good news: Kids tend to be drawn to peers most like themselves. Sociologists call it the principle of homogeneous units. That means that we are usually most comfortable being around people with whom we have the most in common. With rare exception, only in the movies does the youngster from a healthy, happy home environment suddenly sprint into the alley and run off with a drug-addicted motorcycle gang.

"Dr. Don, you almost make it sound like this 'peer pressure' thing is more apt to be driven by my youngster himself than by that group of misfits who meet after school to smoke pot." Bingo! For the most part (I keep making statements like that because kids don't come in boxes—there are always exceptions) kids are drawn to those most like themselves. What was it Mom said about birds of a feather? Right again, Mom.

The decision-making part of your youngster's brain is developing with each passing month (that's encouraging), but it won't be mature until he/she is out of college (college!). That's another way of saying that Joel or Sue is not going to get it right every time. But remember, a kid's most valuable learning comes from trial and error . . . And *error.* So, don't go to pieces when the decisions they make are not the decisions you would have preferred that they make.

Invite that peer group over to your house as often as possible. Get acquainted with them. Rent a video. Order in pizza. Shoot baskets in the driveway. Let some of what you are rub off on them. Baffle your kids with your consistent joy. Distinguish between what you don't like (their music?) and what could be hurtful. Bite your lip about what you don't like; wisely and with respect lead them around the other stuff. Hang with them through this often painful saga when they are likely weighing whether the values they have learned are valuable enough to become their own.

Will your kids be influenced by some blue-haired, multipierced, low-waisted specimen that doesn't shower? Influenced to push the edges perhaps, to test the rules, but be assured that the group does not have the power to overwrite the basic family values you have been working on. Why? Because as you have drawn the boundaries, you have maintained their respect. They know you're real. They know you're on their side. You have positioned yourself in their world as a parent with deep *love and leadership skills.*

The talk on the street is that once kids come to the age of adolescence they are at the mercy of their peers. Not so. You have influenced them for more than 600 weeks. You have lived what you want them to be. You have taught them why every decision they make is important. You have helped them discover the joy of being helpful. You have worked to see that they live in an atmosphere of joy. You have shown them the difference between right and wrong and why the difference matters. You have helped them grasp a vision of why they are here on planet earth. And in doing all this, you have built strong bonds of mutual love and mutual respect. I assure you that in the long term, their peers don't have a chance.

CHAPTER 11

KIDS WHO GLOW IN THE DARK

E. D. Hill, a former Fox News television host and a wonderful writer on building strong families, tells this story, and because she had personal contact with the key player, I believe the story is true.

It was the end of the high school football season, and Neal's[17] school had fielded a team that year that had surprised everyone. The occasion for the story was the final game—for the state championship—the grand finale of high school sports and every student football player's dream.

The game ground on to the fourth quarter, and Neal's team was behind by only three points. The packed stands were electric because one of the teams would go home with the state trophy that would stand in the hallway cabinet forever. The other team would just go home.

One team had the lead but the other team had the ball.

As in every good nail-biter, one team had the lead, but the other team—in this case, Neal's team—had the ball; seconds to go.

The coach sent in the play: a pass play from the shotgun. The quarterback called the play in the huddle: "Neal, wide receiver, go long down the right side. Just short of the goal; hook right. The ball will come over your right shoulder."

The ball is snapped, and, flat out, Neal headed for the goal. He stopped at the three and cut toward the sideline to wait for the spiral that was already arching toward him. It was just beyond his fingertips, but at the last instant he launched his body into the air in a frantic attempt to catch it. Neal and the ball came down together in the end zone. The referee nearest to the play jabbed his hands into the air . . . Touchdown!

Half the fans in the stands went crazy. Neal was an instant hero. His photo would grace the wall beside the trophy cabinet . . . one of the most dramatic catches in the history of the school's sports program . . . to win the state championship. Moms and dads and

---

17 The name I've given him.

coaches and players and the media would replay this athletic marvel as long as there were barbershops and beauty salons where such epics are rehearsed.

But in the midst of the frenzy, a strange thing happened.

But in the midst of the frenzy, a strange thing happened. Neal jumped up holding the ball, broke away from his teammates who were plying him with their attaboys, and ran to the referee, where he excitedly began to explain something. The crowd grew quiet. Neal was explaining that the ball hit the ground and bounced into his arms, and because of where the referee was standing, it only *appeared* as though he had caught it. Only Neal knew the truth. But Neal knew the truth.

The referee changed the call to an incomplete pass; Neal's team lost the game—and the state high school football championship.

Question: Did Neal make the right decision? It's only a game, right?

Remember, every 18-year-old wants to be a hero. We all want to be heroes. But to whom? To the crowd? Sure, but maybe first to ourselves? What value is it to be hailed as a hero by the neighborhood but know in your own heart that you're a phony?

Dr. Hill got in touch with the player I've called Neal, and here is how she reports that contact:

> I read the weekend recap of the game online in a small newspaper, and I called the boy. It was a powerful story of a young man instantaneously making the right choice when it would have been so easy to have done the opposite. When you're a teenage football player, the state championship is the holy grail. His team could have taken the game, and he would have been hailed a hero for scoring the winning touchdown.
>
> No one else knew the ball touched the turf before it

touched his hands. But he knew, and he knew it was not the sportsmanlike way to win despite how desperately he wanted his team to take the championship.

I told him I thought his story was powerful and that I wanted the country to see him, meet him, and learn what a great kid he was. He wanted none of it. He told me he simply did the right thing and told the truth. He didn't expect or want any attention. I wished him well.[18]

Penn State University's legendary coach, Joe Paterno, got it right: "What counts in sports is not the victory," he would say, "but the magnificence of the struggle."

True greatness is a character issue. Not a skill issue. Not a name-in-the headlines issue. Not a picture-on-the-wall issue. Not a most-votes issue. Not a wealth issue. Not the discovery-of-a-powerful-new-vaccine issue. Not a size-of-the-house issue. Not even a she-saved-a-little-kid-from-drowning issue. True greatness is about character.

Character. Maybe we need to define it.

I was impressed but not convinced.

One time a colleague of mine was attempting to convince me about the greatness of a friend of his. He listed some of the man's accomplishments and then ended his inventory by saying, "And he can speak six languages!" I was impressed but not convinced. I've travelled in more than 120 countries, I've lived in Asia and in Europe, and I've studied enough language to know that the ability to speak six effectively is a major accomplishment. *But you can lie in all six.*

Edgar A. Guest, a prolific poet who grew up in Detroit (and who wrote more than 11,000 poems) summarized it:

---

18 E. D. Hill, *I'm Not Your Friend, I'm Your Parent* (Nashville: Thomas Nelson, 2008).

> I have to live with myself, and so
> I want to be fit for myself to know.
> I want to be able, as days go by,
> Always to look myself straight in the eye.

I've searched dictionaries, the Web, and Google, asked friends, explored textbooks, and looked in a host of other places for an adequate definition of character. There are probably some good ones—I just haven't found one. Try to come up with one of your own; you'll see how difficult it is. So for our purposes, here is the definition of "character" as we're using it in this book:

Character: *Those moral qualities that determine how we relate to every situation in life, regardless of the circumstances.*

There's no way in the world I'm going to trade my integrity for two dollars.

Years ago (my kids say I'm using that term a lot lately) I was in a barbershop in Yakima, Washington, getting a haircut. A rather shabbily dressed man came in and told my barber, Jim BoSanko, that he wanted a haircut but he was two dollars short of the posted price. The man said he would pay what he had now and bring the balance in as soon as he could. I will never forget Jim's reply. He said, "Sir, I'll cut your hair, and I believe you'll bring me the rest, because I think you believe just like I do—there's no way in the world I'm going to trade my integrity for two dollars." Or a million?

How do we develop kids with character, kids who are as true to duty as the needle to the pole, whose integrity is not for sale, who will stand for the right though the heavens fall? How do we as parents create an environment that will contribute positively to what kids become so we can watch them internalize unshakable values, such as honesty, morality, and integrity, as though they were part of their DNA?

How do we rear kids like Neal, for whom doing the right thing is never a matter for debate or headlines, no matter the consequences?

As I'm writing this, Fox News is carrying a story that says, "FBI Probing 530 Corporate Fraud Cases." Wouldn't it be great if instead, the headline read something about the titans of corporate America stepping up and saying to our generation, "We may not always make the smartest business decisions, but you can be sure that our decisions will be impeccably honest and as transparent as sunlight"?

As a parent, part of my moral mandate is to help coach a new generation of leaders to that kind of nonnegotiable oath.

How?

I'm sorry, but we've got to move from the lofty and generic to the how-to. And how-to's sometimes pinch.

Situation: You and your family are headed west on I-90; the speed limit is 70 mph. It's a sunny day, the road is clear, the traffic is moving well, and you're in a hurry. Somewhere between 80 and 85 mph feels about right.

From out of nowhere a set of flashing blue lights suddenly dominates your rearview mirror. Gracefully but quickly you ease off the gas pedal and back down to the posted speed limit. To your great relief the lights rush on past.

Whew! Once the lights are out of sight, it's safe to join the drivers around you and resume your former speed.

Question: What lesson did your 9- and 12-year-olds in the backseat just learn? Ouch. You didn't even realize they were watching the speedometer.

Answer: How about "It's OK to break the rules if you don't get caught"? How about "It's OK to do the wrong thing if no one is watching"? How about "That was close . . . you can get away with a lot if you're clever"? How about "As long as everyone else is doing it, it's OK"?

Any possibility some of those same observations may one day drive *their* choices? You may have heard the expression "GIGO: garbage in, garbage out." I'd like to retranslate it and suggest that my version is even more powerful than the original: "GIGO: good stuff in, good stuff out."

Without question, there is no more forceful influence in shaping our kids' integrity than that which they see etched in the hearts of Mom and Dad. Especially if Mom and Dad talk about it; extol its virtues; explain its importance; assume it as a given; expect it of themselves, each other, and the kids; and then illustrate it in every decision, *large and small.*

Large and small. Dad and Mom run a regular booth at the flea market on weekends. They take only cash, and Dad's shirt pocket serves as cash register, so there are no receipts and no way to prove how much they took in or how much profit they made. Simplifies tax time.

Oh, well, it's only 10 bucks and I've got to get home and fix supper.

Large and small. Mom stops by the bank on the way home from picking up Natali at school. She runs in to cash a check, and the teller accidentally gives her one $10 bill too many. Mom discovers it when she gets back to the car. *Oh, well, it's only 10 bucks and I've got to get home and fix supper.*

Large and small. Dad discovers some 2-by-6 studs in the basement that show early signs of termite damage. Rather than replace them, he has his 16-year-old son, Sean, help him sheetrock over them and paint the wall. After all, the house is going on the market in the spring.

Large and small. Big sister, Saundra, is filling out application forms for the college she wants to attend. Her high school employment record is somewhat thin, so dad suggests she might want to enhance it just a tad to include two or three places where she didn't actually work—but might have if she had had a chance.

The most persuasive plank in your youngster's character platform will be the one he or she sees nailed in place at home. Give them much to respect in you.

"But Dr. Don, you're not talking about *my kids'* character development as much as you're talking about *mine.*" Aha! You get it. It's caught *and* taught. You can't sell something you don't own, at least not to your kids; they are, after all, God's little spies.

Character is both taught and caught. So, here is:

TOOL #1:

ABSOLUTE, NONNEGOTIABLE, UNEQUIVOCAL, UNCOMPROMISING, EVEN-WHEN-NO-ONE-IS-WATCHING, UNAPOLOGETIC, TOTALLY CONSISTENT, EVEN-WHEN-PAINFUL INTEGRITY. STARTING AT HOME. IT'S BOTH TAUGHT AND CAUGHT.

TOOL #2:

FEED 'EM THE RIGHT STUFF.

You and I can't remember the first time we heard the statement "You are what you eat." We've heard it often enough to believe it's true, even if we tend to forget it when we're standing in front of the refrigerator with the door open. But it's a truism emotionally and mentally and morally as well as nutritionally.

What are your kids ingesting? Regular meals, I'd bet. Adequate protein, fiber, veggies, fruit. Watch the sugar; easy on the soda pop. You know the drill as well as I. There's a lot of good and bad out there, and we determine to make sure our kids get that which will give them the nutrition they need.

When they are infants and toddlers, we make the nutritional choices for them. (I have a niece who, when she would ask her mother for candy, would be given raisins instead. She was 6 before she learned the difference. Clever mom.) As they grow, we allow them more input into the menu, but with careful coaching. It is our goal that as they are ready to make more choices for themselves, at least two things will have happened. First, they will have developed strong healthy bodies, and second, they will have come to understand the direct line between what they eat and how healthy they are.

You also know that nutrition is not our major concern here. So let's segue with another truism: In the same way that we are what we eat, we become like what we think about; what we ingest mentally determines the health of our character.

Suddenly the subject of *input choices* comes to mind. Television. Books. Magazines. Music. The Web. A whole bunch of external influences fall in this list, don't they? There's lots of good and bad out there. Kids have always had choices, but this is the first generation that has had the menu enhanced by runaway electronics.

Now, I will not presume to set down a list of rules. One size seldom fits all anyway. What I do want to urge is that part of their nurture at our knee must involve helping them learn the consequences of making right—and wrong—choices in the character arena, just as we help them learn to make healthy food choices.

Here's a wonderful idea I thought up that I try to follow: *It is better to light a candle than to curse the darkness.* OK, so I didn't originate it, but it's powerful anyway. (Like many other things you and I enjoy, this one also seems to have come from China.)

So we're looking for ways to develop kids whose characters glow with integrity in a culture steeped in darkness.

Here's one way it might play out . . . At supper one evening, or on a trip in the car, or anywhere there's going to be a little family space, Mom and Dad get into a discussion of a movie they've just seen. Maybe *A Gift of Love: The Daniel Huffman Story.* Or *The Ultimate Gift,* or *Facing the Giants,* or *Letters to God.* One we like a lot is entitled simply *Radio.* These are just five of hundreds of dramatic and very compelling films that are wonderfully entertaining, but that comfortably and almost incidentally teach huge character principles. (I've listed a bunch in the "Resources" section at the back of this book, but of course good new ones are being added all the time. Mine will just serve as samples of what's out there.)

Idea: What about a family night . . . so the family can watch one of these great films together and then have an honest discussion about some of the issues raised; it can be a memorable event at which everyone wins. See: caught and taught.[19]

What we're working on here is creating an environment in which big issues become the focus of some of your family's warmest memories. As it develops it can make television's diet of "fast foods" seem like leftovers. One more suggestion: Begin when they are still young enough that the topics are almost over their heads . . . It's more productive than to wait till it's old hat.

TOOL #3:

INSPIRE THEM TO FIND THE RIGHT KINDS OF HEROES.

Most kids are hero-worshipers to one degree or another. There is no gain in attempting to deny that; we can only try to coach it. It's one thing to be enamored by a celebrity; it's something else to discern the traits that make a celebrity worth fawning over. Charles Barkley understood that when he said, "Just because I dunk a basketball doesn't mean I should raise your kids."

At the beginning of the 2008 baseball season Alex Rodriguez signed with the New York Yankees for a reported $275,000,000 10-year contract. And why not? A-Rod was the world record holder for home runs, and people were willing to pay big bucks to watch him swing for the fences.

What would be your reaction if you logged in to your checking account at the bank and discovered a $27,500,000 deposit—and you knew it was the first of 10? I don't often deal with salary numbers that large, but I think my math is correct. A teen with a $10/week allowance could find that pretty attractive.

When the story broke about Alex's use of performance-enhancing steroids, the talk on the street was, "Well, his place in the record books will need to have an asterisk beside it now because it looks like

---

19 See the "Resources" section beginning on page 132.

his record was chemically augmented." But when it was learned that he had lied on the stand and he was finally backed into a corner and confessed, his name was removed completely.

That *whooshing* sound you heard was the air going out of the Alex Rodriguez balloon. Not the kind of hero you want your teen to chase. But more important, *not the life you want your teen to want to live.* It seems to me that the discussion question here is: How do you think A-Rod felt when he received the accolades but knew he had cheated to get them? Now, there's a good discussion topic for out on the back deck.

Success without honor is an unseasoned dish; it will satisfy your hunger but it won't taste good."

— Joe Paterno

Do you know Kirk Cameron? You do if you have seen *Fireproof*, dubbed the number one inspirational film of 2009. It was produced primarily by volunteers from Sherwood Baptist Church in Albany, Georgia, not your traditional gestation site for blockbuster movies.

Kirk Cameron, who plays the lead, is a professional actor. Both on and off camera he's a very special guy, a devout Christian with exemplary personal standards. For instance, if you have seen the movie, you will remember the emotional reconciliation scene in the firehouse near the end of the film. Kirk and his estranged wife have had their lives changed by an encounter with Jesus Christ, and they meet and embrace between the engines at Station 2.

After an emotional and meaningful hug, the script calls for Kirk and his costar, Erin Bethea, to exchange a passionate kiss. Kirk studied the script and informed the director that his personal morals would not allow him to share that kind of kiss with anyone but his wife. End of discussion.

After some negotiation the problem is solved: Just before the kiss is to be filmed, Erin (Kirk's wife in the movie) steps off camera and

Chelsea (Kirk's real-life wife), with some help from wardrobe, steps in to the scene. You may recall that this sequence in the film is shot from a somewhat distant camera angle so as not to give away the change of personnel. What follows can only be called a real-life passionate kiss.

So, what does that prove—that Kirk Cameron is a prude? No, it illustrates that even in an industry notoriously short on morals (Hollywood consistently does America few favors), there is at least one actor whose personal values are not for sale. H'mmm, a high-visibility young adult celebrity whose morals are not for sale? Now, there's a great while-we're-hiking-through-the-woods discussion topic, too.

Everybody loved Michael. Trim, disciplined, humble, our hero. Every American with red blood was cheering as Michael amazed the world at the 2008 Olympic Games in Beijing and won more first place ribbons—eight—than any person in history. He set a world record in nearly every race he entered. It is my hunch that it will be many Olympics before the accomplishments of Michael Phelps are eclipsed, if ever.

Then Michael's image crashed and burned following a bong-smoking event at the University of South Carolina, which was YouTubed around the world. Kellogg's Cereal was the first sponsor to run for cover. There were others. And whatever you think about the use of pot, Phelps broke the law and perhaps forever tarnished his image as a Pied Piper for our kids. Perhaps more important, the nearly universal adulation turned to sawdust in his mouth.

"If only . . ." is a brutal teacher. More family discussion stuff.

Recent research reveals that people typically lie three times for every 10 minutes of conversation.

In fact, the world is *full* of great discussion material. Seen from this perspective, the whole world is a classroom. Hooks to hang character pictures on are everywhere. And as you and I both read somewhere, character is both caught and taught.

The most persuasive plank in the construction of your youngster's character platform will be the one he or she sees nailed in place at home.

Recent research reveals that people typically lie three times for every 10 minutes of conversation,[20] but I can hear your youngster saying, "Not in my home, we don't!"

Rare kid . . . rare home . . . well done, Mom and Dad.

---

20 MakeYouThink.TV, Ontario, Canada

CHAPTER 12

A BRAND-NEW ENDING

I was standing in front of a huge display of greeting cards looking for one that was just right. Our anniversary was a few days away, and I wanted to find a card that captured exactly how I felt about my longtime bride.

I must have read 50 or maybe a hundred cards, but none of them seemed quite right. No card in the rack could say what I felt. No $10-an-hour homegrown poet sitting at a computer somewhere could put into words the emotions in my heart. A person who had never known Ruthie could not possibly distill into a few lines how I feel about her.

So I made an executive decision: I bought the mushiest card I could find because I wanted something to put on her pillow that night, but I decided I would prepare my own—and it would be from me, from my heart.

I wanted these to be the most beautiful words she had ever heard.

After dinner a couple of nights later we cleared the table, and I told her I had something I wanted to say to her. We sat together on the couch, and I began my spiel. I had poured myself into saying exactly what I was feeling about her, written it down, then more or less memorized it. I wanted to say it just right because I wanted these to be the most beautiful words she had ever heard.

It worked. We both ended up in tears, and we realized anew how very important our love for each other had become.

Envision the God of the universe standing in front of a celestial card rack somewhere, looking for just the right way to say how He felt about us. But nothing impersonal would do. There was no language that could transmit what He wanted to say. So He said to Himself, "I will send my Son—then they'll know."

And He did; and we do.

In the pages of this book I have attempted to be faithful in expressing the principles that God built into family relationships. He is, after all, the Master Designer. Families were His idea. He would not just throw out to us a grand plan and then shout, "Here, follow this if you can."

Rather, He said, "I know you can't do this on your own; you were born with a nature that is both selfish and arrogant. Therefore I will send My Son to illustrate what love means; then I will live within you—at your invitation—and change your nature so you can become like Him."

To many people, becoming a follower of Jesus Christ means having to measure up to an impossibly high standard. It means living by ominous rules that bleed all the joy and freedom out of life. It means keying off of an impossibly austere checklist.

All of those are distorted counterfeits of the real thing. Jesus came to demonstrate how much we are loved. Ponder this: He did not count heaven a place to be desired if *you* were not there. You. So at infinite risk He left there and came here. To love us; to teach us; to show us; to heal us; to change us from the inside into something we could never be on our own.

By our disobedience we forfeited the right to life. He came and paid our penalty and made *forever* again available to us. In His own words, "Greater love has no one than this, that he lay down his life for his friends. *You* are my friends" (John 15:13, 14).

And it was not just a one-time deal. He promises to live within and daily transform us to become like Him. To love like He does. To forgive like He does. To see others as He does. To help us plant a life-transforming love for Him in the hearts of our children.

But Dr. Don, I come from a very dysfunctional family.

Truly an amazing transaction: He offers to take away the penalty that is rightfully ours, and then He extends the invitation to us to live forever. But it's not just about the Sweet Bye and Bye, either; He offers to live within us now—today—so we can take on the character traits He lived when He was here, and then watch as they are instilled in the kids He gives us to love.

"But Dr. Don, I come from a very dysfunctional family. I was abused when I was a kid . . . My Mom and Dad fought till I was a teen, and then he moved out . . . I didn't learn much that I can pass on to my kids." Ah, but the legacy you inherited does not need to be the legacy you leave. Though you cannot go back and make a brand-new start, you can start from now and make a brand-new ending.

You see, the gospel is strong enough to undo all of the damage done by sin. There's a recent Southern Gospel song that says, "There's a Healer Comin' Down the Dusty Road." There is, and it's Jesus! He wants you to invite Him to take up residence in your heart (because He's a Gentleman, He doesn't force His way) so He can help you with your priorities, heal the parts of you that are wounded, and then teach you how to pass those traits on to your family.

Learning to walk in God's story sets us free from the tyranny of small dreams.

A lot of parents work hard to get their kids into the best preschool program, then into the "Gifted and Talented" group at school, then into the finest university; maybe they even offer some help getting started in a career. OK, but that's not our priority; that's not our long-term goal. You see, learning to walk in God's story sets us free from the tyranny of small dreams.

How big is your dream for your kids?

Recently my daughter-in-law, Pam, wrote to me, "Dad, most parents I talk to look back and congratulate themselves on doing a good enough job of parenting as long as their grown kids have jobs, are happily married, aren't in prison, and aren't using drugs."

The really disquieting part of that sentence is the term "good enough." So I have to ask you, How big is your dream for your kids? Is it as big as God's dream for them?

In an earlier chapter we talked about the influence of the peers we associate with. We said that we tend to become like those we spend time with. Let me turn that from horizontal to vertical, from a potential negative to a potentially glorious positive. The more time we spend with God, the more apt we are to take on a strong family likeness. When we spend regular, consistent time reading His Word and talking to Him, the more like His Son we become. Note: This is not just for the spiritual giants among us—those who were somehow born with spiritual genes—it's for *all* of us.

If you haven't already done so, for your sake and for your family's sake, I want to invite you to take a few minutes right now and settle this essential issue. If you have not prayed a prayer like this one, I urge you to read through this one and make it your own right now:

> Dear God, I want to thank You for loving me so much. I want to acknowledge that I am a sinner, born with a sinful nature, and that I can't change that. But I believe that You can. So I invite You to come into my heart and be the Lord of my life. I believe Jesus died on the cross so that my sins can be forever forgiven, and I accept that gift right now. I invite You to live within me and change me to be like Your Son. Amen.

If this is a new journey for you or if it is a renewal of your current journey, I encourage you to bring your calendar to Jesus and ask Him to help you manage your priorities. He will begin by helping you make time every day to read His Word and pray. And remember, we become like those we spend time with; that means it will help if you hook up with a group of folks who are on the same journey you are. We call it church.

I've had this piece in my files for 50 years or more, and I must admit I don't even remember where it came from, as it's tagged "Source Unknown." It's titled "Three Parables," and it's a biographical reflection of three different parents. Paint yourself into one of the pictures:

THREE PARABLES

1st Parable: I took a little child's hand in mine. He and I were to walk together for a while. I was to lead him to the Father. It was a task that overcame me, so awful was the responsibility. I talked to the little child of the Father. I painted the sternness of the Father's face were the child to displease Him.

We walked under tall trees. I said the Father had power to send them crashing down, struck by His thunderbolts. We walked in the sunshine. I told him the greatness of the Father who made the burning, blazing sun.

And one twilight we met the Father. The child hid behind me, he was afraid; he would not look up at the face so loving. He remembered my picture; he would not put his hand in the Father's hand. I was between the child and the Father. I wondered. I had been so conscientious, so serious.

2nd Parable: I took a little child's hand in mine. I was to lead him to the Father. I felt burdened by the multitude of things I was to teach him. We did not ramble; we hastened on from spot to spot.

At one moment we compared the leaves of the different trees, in the next we were examining a bird's nest. While the child was questioning me about it, I hurried him away to chase a butterfly. Did he chance to fall asleep, I wakened him, lest he should miss something I wanted him to see.

We spoke of the Father often and rapidly. I poured into his ears all the stories he ought to know. But we were interrupted often by the coming of the stars, which we must needs study; by the gurgling brook, which we must trace to its source.

And then in the twilight we met the Father. The child merely glanced at Him. The Father stretched out His hand, but the child was not interested enough to take it. Feverish spots burned on his cheeks. He dropped to the ground exhausted and fell asleep. Again I was between the child and the Father. I wondered. I had taught him so many, many things.

3rd Parable: I took a little child's hand in mine to lead him to the Father. My heart was full of gratitude for the glad privilege. We walked slowly. I suited my steps to the short steps of the child.

We spoke of the things the child noticed. Sometimes it was one of the Father's birds; we watched it build its nest, we saw the eggs that were laid. We wondered, later, at the care it gave its young. Sometimes we picked the Father's flowers, and stroked their soft petals and loved their bright colors.

Often we told stories of the Father. I told them to the child and the child told them to me. We told them, the child and I, over and over again. Sometimes we stopped to rest, leaning against the Father's tree, letting His air cool our brows, and never speaking.

And then in the twilight we met the Father. The child's eyes shone. He looked up lovingly, trustingly, eagerly into the Father's face; he put his hand into the Father's hand. I was for the moment forgotten. I was content.

I WANT YOU TO MEET MY FRIEND...

I am deeply grateful to my friend, John Rosemond, for his help and encouragement in the writing of Rare Kids; Well Done. Few people in our nation's history have written more, spoken to more parents, or had a greater impact on America's families than he.

John's newspaper column—which he has written weekly for almost 30 years—appears in nearly 250 newspapers nationwide, with an estimated readership of 10 million. Most of the 14 or so books he has written on parenting have become best sellers. He speaks more than 150 times each year to parent groups, educators, churches, synagogues, and corporations. Among his media appearances are Good Morning America, The View, Real Time With Bill Maher, CBS's The Early Show, The Dennis Prager Show, and a host of others.

During the time this book was in preparation it was my privilege to become well acquainted with John. We just clicked. While attending a seminar he was conducting, I found his message to be so compelling that I wanted to know how I could help get it to a wider audience. Over the next few months I earned certification in John Rosemond's Leadership Parenting Institute and was subsequently invited to become its administrator. It has been a stimulating ride.

John has had a profound influence on my own understanding of how parents can raise kids who are apt to become respectful, responsible, and obedient. Many of the concepts in this book have grown out of insights I received from listening to him speak and reading what he has written. I am forever grateful that God permitted our paths to cross.

Perhaps his greatest influence on my life has been his unflinching commitment to the ageless truths of Scripture and the wisdom God has included there to help us be the parents He wants us to be. That allegiance brings an inspired integrity to his mission.

On another of these pages I have listed some of his writings. I invite you to take advantage of that list and get acquainted with the books that are listed there. I promise you that every title listed is a family-changer.

Learn more about the man and his mission at www.rosemond.com.

[THANK YOU]

PICTURES HANGING
IN MY PERSONAL HALL OF FAME

I am so indebted to a busload of people for their help in getting this project to completion. First has to be Lori Peckham, perhaps one of the world's greatest living editors. Thanks, Lori, for bringing both your expertise and your heart to the task.

Emily Harding, designer extraordinaire, who took words on a page and made them a work of art. Emily, you are the best.

Ruthie, love of my life, my best critic, best friend and cheerleader – thank you for your penchant for excellence.

John Rosemond, coach and friend. Thanks for your deep insights into the development of effective parenting skills. I suspect that few people in history have had the positive impact on the family that you have. And on me.

And so many others – my kids, Jerry and Randy, who provided many of the delicious vignettes in the book. Alicia Patterson who helped a lot with advice in the early stages. Tom Lighthall who read early chapters with a trained eye and gave me courage. Dr. Tracy Edwards, Christian physician and valued friend who helped me with some tricky places in the manuscript. And a thousand families through the years who have invited me into the inner circle of their lives and allowed me the privilege of watching them work their way toward joy.

And finally, to a loving God who long ago gave us a Book and put in it everything we need to get life right. We hope You are pleased to look at us and call us Rare Kids; Well Done.

[RESOURCES]

BOOKS

My friend and colleague, John Rosemond, has probably the strongest and most consistent library of books available on the subject of parenting. Most are best-sellers. Here is a list of my favorites from his pen. All are available from his website, www.rosemond.com or from Amazon.com

- *Parenting By the Book* – 2007

- *The Well-Behaved Child* – 2009

- *Teen-Proofing* – 2000

- *Family Building* - 2005

- *The Diseasing of America's Children* – 2009

- *The New Six-Point Plan for Raising Happy, Healthy Children* – 2006

- *Toilet Training Without Tantrums* – 2010

- *Making the "Terrible" Twos Terrific* – 1993

- *Ending the Homework Hassle* – 1990

- *John Rosemond's New Parent Power* – 2001

MORE BOOKS

- *The Dangerous Book for Boys*, Conn and Hal Iggulden, Harper Collins, 2007. Challenges today's protective parent to let their kids be kids. A fascinating book.

- Have *a New Kid by Friday*, Kevin Leman, 2008

- *Making Children Mind Without Losing Yours*, Kevin Leman, 2005

- *Dr Kevin Leman LIVE! Straight Talk on Parenting, 2010*

A/V

Understanding that levels of acceptance vary greatly between individuals we have chosen videos that carry powerful stories which are produced for conservative tastes. These are only suggestive of good conversation-starters for your family.

- The Blind Side – 2010

- The Christmas Card - 2007

- Facing the Giants – 2007

- Fireproof - 2009

- Flywheel - 2003

- Letters to God - 2010

- Radio – 2004

- The Ultimate Gift - 2007

[CONTACT]

CONTACT US FOR

- additional copies of the book

- quantity discounts

- to book Dr Don to speak to your parent group

- and to see other Rare Kids resources
  www.RareKidsWellDone.com

FOLLOW DR. DON'S WEEKLY BLOG AT
www.RareKidsWellDone.com/blog.

CONTACT THE AUTHOR AT
DrDon@rarekids.net

[NOTES]

RARE KIDS; WELL DONE

[NOTES]

[NOTES]

[NOTES]

_____

_____

_____

_____

_____

_____

_____

_____

_____

_____

_____

_____

_____

_____

_____

_____

_____

_____

RARE KIDS, WELL DONE

[NOTES]

_____

_____

_____

_____

_____

_____

_____

_____

_____

_____

_____

_____

_____

_____

_____

_____

_____

[NOTES]

[NOTES]

[NOTES]

[NOTES]